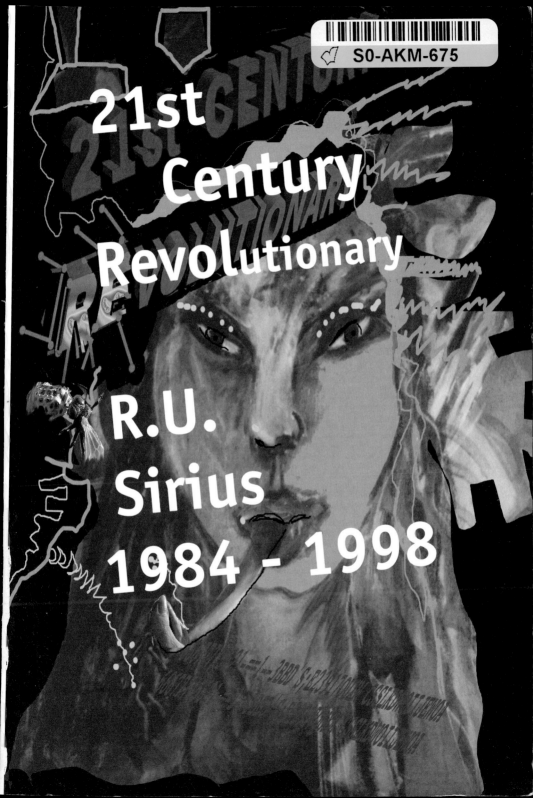

21st Century Revolutionary

R.U. Sirius

1984 - 1998

Title: "21st CENTURY REVOLUTIONARY"
"R.U. SIRIUS 1984-1998"

Author: R. U. Sirius
Designer: Eve Berni
ISBN: 90-76207-51-8
© 1999 by Ken Goffman
Design: © 1999 by Eve Berni

Published by:
FRINGECORE
P.O. Box 165
2600 Berchem 1
Belgium
www.fringecore.com

Permissions to reprint:

"Fleshware", "Transmutationism:
an Extropunkian's Strange Pursuit,"
"Dana Beal and Friends in Search of the Holy Grail,"
"The Dope Fiend Manifesto," and "The Tyranny of Hip"
from 21.C
"It's Better to be Inspired than Wired" from St. Martin's Press
"The Road Behind: Bill Gates" from ARTFORUM International
"What About Cyberdelia?" from Mark Dery
"We are Ducahmpians of the World" from World Art
"R.U. Sirius' Guide to the Alternative 70s" from bOING bOING

Thanks to Per Eidspjeld for the backcover photos, Heide Foley and
Jay Cornell for design advise.

**This book is dedicated to the memory of
Anita Hoffman, Kathy Acker and Timothy Leary**

INTRODUCTION:
MY LIFE AS A WRITER   **page 4**

CHAPTER ONE:
REVOLTING! DEVELOPMENTS page 9
1996-1998

CHAPTER TWO:
TRIPPING AND FALLING OVER page 83
THE (NEW) EDGE
     1984-1992

CHAPTER THREE: **page 129**
CLOWN PRINCE OF THE
DIGITAL REVOLUTION
     1993-1995

I never got any approval for anything other than taking out the garbage for my mom and dad until I won a SUNY (State University of New York) Short Story Award in 1979.

I was 27 years old and a junior in college. I'd never been able to stomach or keep a job or even *think* about the idea of a career. As an adolescent I'd been dimly aware that right outside my small coterie of friends was an entire culture of kids who knew they would soon have to do something to "make a living." And they were all making their preparations. From the working class "rats" down in the basement of the high school where they learned "industrial machine shop" to the upper class 60s-liberal collegiate kids to whom I occasionally sold bogus drugs, they had come to some kind of internal accommodation with reality.

But I don't recall any of my high school friends wanting to *be* anything except stoned... or perhaps naked, stoned, and running down the street with the Police Chief's head on a stick! I certainly never thought about "being a writer," although I did write most of a small underground paper (xerox) that I distributed for free around the school. (It became an instant hit when the Principal announced that anybody caught with a copy would be suspended).

In college, where I was finally stumbling towards a Master's Degree in "Fiction Writing," they told me that writers get up every morning and spend hours in front of the typewriter (Word processor to you young'uns.) I told them I was *not* a writer. They told me that creativity is 1% inspiration and 99% perspiration. I told them, "What you see is what you get." As part of my Master's program, I was working on a novel. It was called "Dr. Fuck or the Humorous Permutations of Human Flesh and Blood in the DNA Age." I wrote about 100 pages, single-spaced. It was, according to my advisor, "a gallery of grotesques." But where was it going? I didn't know. I didn't have an ending... or even a middle. Well, let's see. It's a story about wacky psychedelic Californians in some kind of absurdist hightech/biotech future. I need more information to complete my fiction. I know! I'll take the generous $5,000 student loan that the State of New York proffered on me for attending the summer semester and hop on a plane for San Francisco.

I did just that. I didn't have flowers in my hair, but I did have a sheet of acid and a couple of grams of hashish in my boot. (And I'm still paying off the interest on my student loans.) And thereby hangs the tale. Once in "San Francisco" (I wound up in Berkeley, to be precise), whenever I would sit down to write, all that would come out was this "things to do list": 1) Start the neopsychedelic movement 2) Start a neopsychedelic magazine. 3) Start a neopsychedelic band. They say that two out of three ain't bad. Indeed. Instead of finishing my fiction, I *lived* it.

I have not changed much. While I desperately would love to make a decent living "being a writer" my basic gut impulse is to *be* naked, stoned and running down the street with Jesse Helms' head on a stick. Joseph Campbell said follow your bliss and the money will take care of itself. How much do I hear for the head of Jesse Helms?

It hasn't been all bliss, or even 100% uncompromisingly authentic, but starting with the act of publishing the neopsychedelic magazine *High Frontiers* in 1984, I have been able to *almost* slide by being R.U. Sirius; zeitgeist savant, digital iconoclast, and truth ranter. And as far as my "career" goes, I have had the following major league near-misses: my own television show on PBS, a music career involving five CD's released by Trent Reznor's Nothing Records, and a highly lucrative lecture tour of Europe. But in the end, I've earned my living—such as it is—primarily as a writer. And am I happy with this turn of events? FUCK YOU!!!!!

CHAPTER ONE: REVOLTING! DEVELOPEMENTS
1996-1998 10

It's Better to be Inspired than Wired: the R.U. Sirius 12
Interview (Jon Lebkowsky, CTHEORY 1996)

Tactical Toilet Training: R.U. Sirius Interviewed 20
  by Pit Schultz (NETTIME 1996)

Fleshware: Rudy Rucker Interview 24

The Road Behind: Bill Gates
(ARTFORUM International, 1996) 29

Timothy Francis Leary 1920-1996 32
(Hotwired 1996, Mondo 2000, 1996)

TransMutationism: an ExtroPunkian's Strange Pursuit 35
  (21•C, 1996)

What About Cyberdelia: R.U. Sirius Vs. Mark Dery 37
(Hotwired 1996)

Empathy For the She-Devil: R.U. Loves Courtney 45
(Might, 1996)

We Are Duchampians of the World 46
(World Art, 1997)

Why I'm REVOLTING! (REVOLTING!, 1997). 48

Just Say Nothing:
R.U. Sirius Deconstructs the Philosophical Depths of the Now and
Near Future Digital Generations
(The Site, 1997) 51

Dana Beal and Friends In Search of the Holy Grail
(21•C, 1997) 55

The Dope Fiend Manifesto
(21•C, 1997, Utne Reader 1998) 58

John Perry Barlow Debriefed -
(Mondo 2000, 1998). 60

The TechnoSurrealist Manifesto (DisInformation, 1998) . . . 67

The Revolution ®   (DisInformation, 1998) 71

Technology is a Trickster God: 79
an Interview with Erik Davis (Salon, 1998)

CHAPTER TWO: TRIPPING AND FALLING OVER (THE) NEW EDGE   1985-1992 82

Coming Out of Left Field: an Interview with
Gracie & Zarkov   (High Frontiers, 1985). 86

The CIA, LSD and the Occult: an Interview with Martin Lee
(with Severe Tire Damage, High Frontiers, 1987). 96

Is There Any Escape From Stupid?
with Don Joyce and Mark Hosler of Negativland
(with Stephan Ronan, Mondo 2000, 1990). 102

Civilizing the Electronic Frontier:
an Interview with Mitch Kapor & John Perry Barlow of the
Electronic Frontier Foundation
(with David Gans, Mondo 2000, 1990). 120

CHAPTER THREE : CLOWN PRINCE OF THE DIGITAL REVOLUTION 1993-1995 129

R.U. Sirius Guide to the Alternative '70s
(bOING bOING, 1993). 132

Kathy Acker: Where Does She Get Off?
(io, 1993) 136

Pomo to Go: a User's Guide to Trendy French Intellectuals
(With Carmen Hermosillo, Wired 1994). 141

Cyberpunk Lite: Gibson & Sirius Wax Laconic
(Unpublished, 1994) 146

The Tyranny of Hip   (21•C, 1995). 153

A Guy With a Backache:
01 (1995) 155

REVOLTING! Developments:

CHAPTER ONE

Chapter Introduction

As you may note, this collection starts at the end and then doubles back to the beginning. Why? Well, I ain't fuckin' Gore Vidal or Norm Mailer. The trajectory of the career of R.U. Sirius is of limited interest to most of the *People* or even *Wired*-reading public. I've got to put my best face forward so you'll be interested in going back and examining the historic progression. I even thought of running this chapter backwards, since the stuff from 1998 is even better than the stuff from 1996. In fact, you can go ahead if you want and start from the back of this chapter and work your way to the front of it.

It's passing ironic, since my career—or at least my media coverage and freelance income—is in a tailspin. Why does the world work like that? Not because of you, dear reader. But probably because of your dumb fuckin' brother Chuckie... er, that is... one of the motivations for this book is that so much of this stuff has gone unnoticed, barely finding its way out of Australia or the cutout bin at your local book shop, if any. Oh well. I am not the first—nor will I be the last—writer whose best work winds up in some inexplicable void. And no, I'm not feeling sorry for myself... just making conversation, ok? About the time the doorknob broke. Like that.

Listen. The narrative trajectory of this book—the bits of introductory material that surround the bulk of this collection—will be about my "career." I don't know why. It's just coming out that way. Sure, it's self-indulgent. I could be talking about the cultural environment and influences, the trends that motivated the text. Forget it. There's one cultural influence in publishing. No, *not* money. Oprah. If Oprah Winfrey likes your book, you're a success. If not, you're screwed. The mainstream book industry should simply run all book proposals past Oprah to see what she wants to read, and not waste the time of other authors, whose books are being buried, sometimes within days, by a hysterical publishing environment that makes Wall Street look like a zen monastery.

My work in 1996-1997 is primarily about rage. By 1998, my rage is tempered by love and transcendent humor thanks to a gal named Eve.

The R.U. Sirius Interview:

It's Better to be Inspired than Wired

*The "Republican Revolution" of 1994 used Libertarian rhetoric to attack government programs for the poor. This put me into a spin that eventually caused me to make a sharp left turn. When the Electronic Frontier Foundation (*Wired *insiders for the most part) met with Newt Gingrich's PFF organization and they all held hands and prayed for the* devolution of the welfare state, *I felt ill.*

CTHEORY (World Wide Web)   April 1996

——————————————————————————————————

by Jon Lebkowsky

CLOWN PRINCE OF THE DIGITAL COUNTERCULTURE

The evolution of a bohemian, technohip subculture within the vibrant and elastic digital culture of today was mediated by two important events. One was the opening of the Internet. The other was the appearance of *Mondo 2000.*

The early Internet derived much of its ambiance from a strange hybrid of 60s counterculture and 80s libertarianism. *Mondo 2000,* a glossy periodical that evolved from an earlier neopsychedelic zine, incorporated this sociopolitical sensibility and blended it with their own peculiar sense of post-punk irreverence, drugged-up pranksterism, and high style. The result was a new cultural trend, or at least the media-generated illusion of one.

It was 1989. Computers were seen as tools of High Geekdom. *Mondo,* however, portrayed the new technology as sexy, hip, and powerfully subversive. And as Captain Picard might say, they made it so.

It was Bart Nagel's unique computer-enhanced graphic style that pushed *Mondo 2K* over the top, making it something of a phenomenon in the early 90s. However, the real meat was in the cheerfully irreverent exploration of nascent technoculture and the evolving computer underground from the perspective of the writer/editors, whose handles were R.U. Sirius, St. Jude, and Queen Mu. Besides displaying strangeness and charm, early Mondo was the only popular representation of the hacker ethic, described by author Andrew Ross as "libertarian and crypto-anarchist in its right-to-know principles and its advocacy of decentralized knowledge. [It] asserts the basic right of users to free access to all information. It is a principled attempt, in other words, to challenge the tendency to use technology to form information elites." [*Technoculture* 116]

Despite being non-technical, *Mondo 2000*'s original Editor-in-Chief, the iconoclastic prankster R.U. Sirius, saw clearly the broad implications of the hacker ethic and incorporated it into his bag of tricks. He began hanging out on the WELL, at that time a little-known Bay Area conferencing system that attracted writers, hackers, artists, poets, and publishers from all over the world. He started a topic on *Mondo 2000* in the Hacking conference on the WELL, which evolved into the once-vibrant, now defunct Mondo 2000 conference.

In 1993, Sirius split from *Mondo 2000*. Since then, he's contributed his increasingly acerbic scribblings to publications ranging from *ARTFORUM International* to *Wired* to *Esquire Japan*. In 1994, he recorded an unreleased album called *IOU Babe* for Trent Reznor's Nothing Records with his conceptual-art rock band MV Inc. (formerly called Mondo Vanilli). He has also co-authored two books with St.Jude, *Cyberpunk Handbook: the Real Cyberpunk Fakebook* (Random House), and *How to Mutate and Take Over the World* (Ballantine).

As this interview was completed, Sirius told me about his new website, called "The Mutate Project", that includes a public forum on "how to conduct a guerrilla war against the censorship of the Internet... and other stuff." However sirius this may sound, you can bet it's always somewhat tongue-in-chic.

MONDO TO THE CORE

CTHEORY: Did *Mondo 2000* just cycle out? Or do you think, in a perfect world, you could've held the cultural edge and continued to produce quality content?
RU Sirius: Mondo had its moment on the tip of the wave. But I think that a certain combination of our editors and art people could have launched the truly corrosive assault on computer and media culture that was implicit in Mondo at its best. I think it's silly to chase the edge. It's much more interesting to explode it... as well as the mainstream. It's better to be inspired than wired.

CTHEORY: When you're associated with the neophile fringe there's that expectation that you'll always be remaking reality, though. Finding the next frontier...
RU: Right. But I don't worry so much about the "neophile fringe" or the cult of newness, believe it or not. I'm more interested in passion and philosophy, sex and subversion... you know... those old-fashioned values. This macho sort of posturing about being the fastest, most technohip, way-ahead person around gets really tiresome. It was sort of funny to me as the *Mondo 2000* thing got going that some people really thought that I should feel ashamed because I'm not an authentic hacker. Really, who gives a fuck? I'm not an auto mechanic either. I just feel compelled to do various forms of communication and make art about the things that intrigue me.

CTHEORY: It seems that *Mondo* tried to be digital culture while at the same time slam dunking it.
RU: Yes! My book *How To Mutate & Take Over the World* does that also. *HR&TOW* is both the next stage and my personal kiss off to the so-called cyberculture. We were always horribly ambiguous. Even our hortatory, wild-eyed, faux-utopian opening statement from the first issue (which, incidentally, the academic types insist on keeping in circulation as proof of our naiveté), was more an exercise in poetic extravagance then something to live and die by. So I rode the Virtual Reality hype and the smart drugs hype, but I also made a lot of cynical statements about them. Throughout the early 90s, I repeated the line "I'd rather watch *Ren and Stimpy* on caffeine than experience virtual reality on smart drugs" in all my lectures and interviews, to try to detach from excessive identification with disappointing infant tech-

nologies. It's a very true statement, by the way. But ironic distance also quickly becomes banal... and that spells exhaustion. Let's not talk about exhaustion. What can you say, really?

CTHEORY: There have been many rumors about your reasons for splitting from *Mondo* in 1993. What's the real, unexpurgated story?

RU: I split primarily because I wasn't the one at the controls, and I could feel the thing spinning out of control and couldn't do anything about it. Unless you were inside *Mondo,* you couldn't possibly understand what it was like. Read *Alice In Wonderland* and the collected works of Kafka as though they were instruction manuals for how to succeed in business, for starters. I'm not interested in magnifying the details though. I love everybody involved.

You know, only an absolute nut would have supported and helped to create *Mondo* 2000 when it started in 1989 so what the hell. And I'm a complete lunatic myself so I can only be thankful. I've always been through the looking glass.

CYBERPUNK: THREAT, MENACE, OR MARKETING CONCEPT?

CTHEORY: Speaking of the past, let's talk about the c-word. *Mondo 2000* was a focus of a superficial "movement" that called itself cyberpunk, after the literary genre. But like *Mondo,* it seems to be gasping for breath. The sf writers who were reluctantly responsible for the meme seem kind of relieved. But you released a book called *The Cyberpunk Handbook* in 95. What's your take?

RU: Bruce Sterling didn't want to have anything to do with it when we interviewed him back in 89. He said he was "taking down the neon sign." All labels are just conveniences and anybody who takes them too seriously is a fool. But the compulsive need to jettison a label might just be one aspect of taking it too seriously. Does the label help you to communicate a certain aesthetic or a set of generally held beliefs and attitudes? Are you searching for a new label just because somebody told you that it wasn't hip to use this one anymore?

I'm terribly trendy myself. I'm easily pressured by the tyranny of hip. So I had resolutely forsworn against the use of "cyber" in any form. But then I was offered a mercenary opportunity by Random House to assault the cyberpunk concept - in other words to help write a book called *The Cyberpunk Handbook*. It was their idea. I wanted to get the advance for the book and then change the title, but by the time we got the advance, Jude had written a whole bunch of great stuff about cyberpunks. And you know, fuck 'em if they can't take a joke.

CTHEORY: Cyberpunk was really just a marketing term from the word go.

RU: Art movements usually are. Gibson, Sterling and company saw an opportunity to market a genre, which is how you move product in a dense media culture. People need the various classifications and subclassifications to know where to go, because there's too much stuff. The cool thing about the cyberpunk genre is that it's been pretty elastic. Pat Cadigan, Rudy Rucker, *Mondo 2000,* ravers, SRL, underground hackers, Gibson, Leary... it provided a pretty big tent for people to hawk their wares from.

CTHEORY: But cyberpunk seems to be dying now as a marketing concept. We thought we were in on the ground floor and, next thing we knew, we were buried under the basement–coopted by a larger commercial mainstream. The big ques-

tion seems to be whether the Internet will become completely corporatized. And if it does, will there be alternative channels?

RU: Well, it's a legal matter now. A heavily-censored net will make any sort of alternativeness difficult. But there's no easy division. Push comes to shove, the media corps have to sell our pre-packaged little revolts-into-style for us because there's a consumer demand that isn't going to go away. Things are too unsatisfactory and people need to spit it up. Or, in other words, the corporate sponsors will want to put their little logos on everything.

CTHEORY: A favorite example being William S. Burroughs in a Nike ad.

RU: You said it! Would I do a Nike ad? I *would!* And does that weaken my stance? It *does!*

CTHEORY: And do you care?

RU: I *don't!* Really, heroism is a spectator sport. Fuck spectators. Anybody who doesn't factor a need to pay rent and to have pleasures into whatever expectations they have of anybody else can go to fuck. I hate expectations of any kind.

CTHEORY: Subversion never completely succeeds but neither does the attempt to squash it.

RU: Subversion by its nature parasitizes whatever it attempts to subvert. But subversion isn't really subversive any more. I mean, you can do the most outrageous shit, and people's ability to react is just flattened. The greatest hope for subversives is William Bennett and the Christian Coalition and all that. They are trying their best to make subversion subversive again... god bless 'em!

Trapped in a World He Never Made

CTHEORY: You seem to be into paradox. Leading cyberculture while slamming it, practicing raw capitalism while critiquing it in the process. This paradox seems to run through much of the culture jamming stuff.

RU: Well, anybody who doesn't believe that we're trapped hasn't taken a good look around. We're trapped in a sort of mutating multinational corporate oligarchy that's not about to go away. We're trapped by the limitations of our species. We're trapped in time. At the same time identity, politics, and ethics have long turned liquid. It seems that what we have, at least among the sort of hip technophile population, is an experimental attitude. An experimental attitude is one of not knowing, otherwise it's not really experimental. Also, most people try so hard to put their best face forward, right? I mean, if you're writing a righteous political statement on Monday and you're hyping your ass and talking to the lawyers on Tuesday, you're not going to emphasize Tuesday. You're not going to emphasize your own corruption. Except I tend to, because the deal is what's real. If I can make one claim, it's that I'm the most anti-purist motherfucker around.

CTHEORY: I was talking to former FCC commissioner Nicholas Johnson at a party last night. He was talking about the corporate monopolization of media. If five major corporations control all but the tiniest media channels, then they control the flow of information. In an information economy, that's the flow of life. That's why the corporate/government interests want to control the Internet. To them, it's just one of the several media distribution channels. Zines and pirate

15

media may continue to exist, but they're nothing against the corporate powers.
RU: There's some complicated dynamics there, between corporate interests, government interests, popular interests, and individual liberties that aren't so easily sorted out, but I'll say this from my little corner of the universe. If you have laws against "obscenity" and "indecency" in an open channel like the net, you've effectively silenced the non-mainstream, non-conforming voice because, sooner or later, this is the medium where it all converges. That's not some kind of *Wired*-style technophilia, that's just a fact of life. Sooner or later it all converges around an extension of telephony. Now, corporate media is a tremendous sponsor of alternativeness, but they can survive without it. Or they can pressure artists to tone it down. So it's the independents who are going to be crushed by this, as usual.

However, the net is a terrific environment for guerrilla warfare. It's a great jungle in which to hide and from which to make attacks. And your attacks are by nature communicative. That's what a big chunk of *HTM&TOW* is about.
CTHEORY: I think that effective "guerrilla actions" in a mediated environment will have terrific subtlety. Have you any examples of this kind of poetic terrorism from your own work?
RU: I hope that *HTM&TOW* is the answer to that question. One idea we propagate is that media hackers have to be really fucking great entertainers. That's the key. When you pirate television time, for instance, it should be such a fun thing that people are waiting at their VCRs for the next one.

I remember having an underground paper in high school. As soon as the Principal announced over the loudspeaker that kids weren't allowed to have it, everybody wanted one. As soon as the kids saw that it was playful and funny, they wanted the next one. Of course, adults tend to view anything that isn't dull with suspicion, which is a problem.

Bigger than Satan? R.U. Sirius for Anti-Newt!
CTHEORY: You clearly embrace a lot of contradictions. But what is it that you hope to accomplish? Is there, in any sense, a positive project?
RU: The R.U. Sirius project has always been largely about re-energizing the forgotten "ideology" of the 60s revolt, primarily the notion of post-scarcity liberation. I hesitate in tying myself to the 60s mast, but we're not talking Paul McCartney or George McGovern here.

OK... post-scarcity was basically a premature post-industrial vision of a cybernetic culture in which alienated labor and scarcity was all but eliminated by technology. This had an enormous influence, sometimes explicit and sometimes subterranean. If you go back and investigate the writings of the Yippies, the diggers, Daniel Cohn-Bendit, who led a near revolution in France in 1968, and various other political radicals, the ones that didn't get absorbed into old fashioned Marx-Leninism, you find this theme over and over again. The machines of loving grace.

This isn't utopian, by the way. I'm anti-utopian. I don't believe in totalizing philosophies or perfect happy endings. But it could be hella better than it is now.
CTHEORY: This is like [anarchist subculture figure] Bob Black's vision of ludic society.

RU: Actually we're in a very perverted version of a ludic society, in the sense that what's driving technological evolution is shifting from warfare to information, communications, and entertainment... better games, greater bandwidth, film projects the size of military invasions and entertainment corporations the size of medium nation states.

CTHEORY: An extension of the Japanese postwar economy.

RU: Yes. Big business with everybody so seriously dedicated to play that they never get a chance to...

CTHEORY: Play is work.

RU: Right. In so many ways, our society explicitly strives to be the direct opposite of the ideal. It's pretty funny. On the other hand, this speed-of-light hell-on-wheels that we're living in seems to make for a lot of creative energy. There's something to be said for the stress that makes us all want to kill each other and make really cool web pages.

CTHEORY: Notions like the end of work and scarcity are very obscure right now. Why do you think they're relevant?

RU: All you have to do is look at the situation to realize that it's the only relevant political position for anybody who isn't rich. As the result of automation and internationalization, the economic power of ordinary people, which used to reside in the "working class," has completely disappeared—which, incidentally, is why a lot of people have little reason to be thrilled by the relative democratization of media communications that *Wired* and *Mondo* have touted. Also, the virtual economy has overwhelmed the "real" economy of goods and services... at the cutting edge of capitalism, you're in a pure "transacting" economy of derivatives, currency exchanges, options and so forth that has displaced economics. Networked electronic trading is very much its own unique ecology. "Money" is being made not in the investing itself but on the abstraction of the transacting of conceptual wealth. Tremendous profits can be conjured from the consensual hallucination that a transaction that doesn't necessarily have to happen might accumulate (for example) interest at a later date.

The important thing here is that not only doesn't capitalism require as many workers, it doesn't require as many consumers. An economy that trades in pure abstraction is self-sufficient. It can satisfy itself building hallucinatory fortunes that can be cashed in for ownership of property and advanced techno-toys for your wired elite. It's all just bits and bytes really. It's a trick. But it conflates nicely with the logic of late capitalism which is to eliminate that which is superfluous, in other words the formerly working class people who are no longer needed as workers or consumers. That's what downsizing is about... killing the poor. This is not even a slight exaggeration. This is exactly the trajectory of late capitalism, and specifically of the Republican revolution.

Anyway, grant me that we're in a situation where workers are increasingly superfluous. I don't have the figures on hand, but some extraordinary percentage of those people who are employed work for temp agencies. Hazel Henderson told me that 60% of the American people are either unemployable, unemployed, working temp, or working without benefits or job security. A week after she said that, I saw Labor Secretary Robert Reich on television saying more or less the same thing, but the figure was 70%. But a recent poll shows that something like 95% identify themselves as middle class. Hah! They're not middle class.

What you actually have, in vaguely Marxist terminology, is an enormous lumpenproletariat. In other words, non-working or barely-working poor. I mean, this is the most oppressed country in the Western world according to all kinds of statistics. The Reagan Revolution turned the average American into a citizen of the third world. And here comes Newtie to finish the job.

People identify with the middle class though... they're temp workers with televisions, CD players, and hip clothes and hairstyles.

The only alternative to a world of human refuse, serfs and slaves abandoned by an increasingly self-sufficient corporate cyber/media oligarchy is a revolution of this lumpenproletariat (the formerly working class), based not in neo-Luddite refusal but in desire, a desire to live. Which means that the essentials should be given away free, unconditionally. This notion is of course completely in opposition to the current political discourse, and probably goes against every instinct in, say, the average *Wired* reader's brain. I'd like them to just think of me as the anti-Newt.

Cyberculture (a meme that I'm at least partly responsible for generating, incidentally) has emerged as a gleeful apologist for this kill-the-poor trajectory of the Republican revolution. You find it all over *Wired*—this mix of chaos theory and biological modeling that is somehow interpreted as scientific proof of the need to devolve and decentralize the social welfare state while also deregulating and empowering the powerful, autocratic, multinational corporations. You've basically got the breakdown of nation states into global economies simultaneous with the atomization of individuals or their balkanization into disconnected sub-groups, because digital technology conflates space while decentralizing communication and attention. The result is a clear playing field for a mutating corporate oligarchy, which is what we have. I mean, people think it's really liberating because the old industrial ruling class has been liquefied and it's possible for young players to amass extraordinary instant dynasties. But it's savage and inhuman. Maybe the wired elite think that's hip. But then don't go around crying about crime in the streets or pretending to be concerned with ethics.

It's particularly sad and poignant for me to witness how comfortably the subcultural contempt for the normal, the hunger for novelty and change, and the basic anarchistic temperament that was at the core of *Mondo 2000* fits the hip, smug, boundary-breaking, fast-moving, no-time-for-social-niceties world of your wired megacorporate info/comm/media players. You can find our dirty fingerprints, our rhetoric, all over their advertising style. The joke's on me.

CTHEORY: Clearly there's a fragmentation of community and dissolution of soul. We all sort of slid into it as cyberfoo was co-opted and the Internet was transformed into digital Las Vagueness, but what are you going to do? Do you have a political agenda or a performance agenda?

RU: My main agenda is to explode constricting illusions, whether it's bourgeois propriety, expectation, shame over sexuality, or the money system. Also, in Freudian terms, I'm at war with the cultural superego in favor of the disencumberment of the libido, the id, and the ego... definitely in that order—which connects me to the surrealist and dadaist traditions. Anyway, I don't acknowledge any separation between a political agenda, a performance agenda, a pop agenda, a theoretical agenda, a radical agenda, a survival agenda, a sexual agenda...

My activities right now include getting attention for the book *How To Mutate & Take Over the World* which I believe is an actual act of sabotage against the plans of big media/technology business, for reasons that aren't immediately obvious. The book announces itself as an act of sabotage on the surface, and fails as that, again on the surface. Wait and see how it unfolds.

At the same time, I believe that I'm finally prepared to give expression to a complete alternative, revolutionary philosophy for the next decade. I'm prepared to deal with both deconstructions and visionary alternatives regarding the money system, cyborgization, virtualization, media, violence and violent media and art, censorship, uncertainty, extropianism or the transcendence of ordinary life, sociobiology, race, gender, sexuality, drugs, individualism and community. I'm ready to put forth a digital age politic that embraces the goals of both liberalism and libertarianism. I believe this will come together with the help of collaborators over the next year or two, and will be presented on The Mutate Project web page.

Nobody has exploded the meaning of the money system or really produced a visionary sociopolitical agenda for a post-industrial economy. It can be done. And I'll do it, with some help.

You know, I see all these media and software people making and spending millions and millions of dollars, and all of these millions of dollars being pissed away on mediocre films, mediocre magazines, pea-brained rock bands, stupid web sites—it makes me sick. Give me one million fucking dollars and I'll bring you major cultural and political change within four years. The few people who really know about *Mondo 2000* and what we did with very tiny resources will know that I'm being megalomaniacal but I may be right, everybody else will think I'm just being megalomaniacal. But I've grown a lot since *Mondo 2000*. Get me behind the wheel of another vehicle and *Wired* will be eating my dust. I want to be bigger than Satan.

Tactical Toilet Training:
Five Questions to RU Sirius from Pit Schultz:

This interview took place in end of May 1996 via email and refers to "The R.U. Sirius Interview: It's Better to be Inspired than Wired by Jon Lebkowsky" which appeared in CTHEORY, Special Edition 1.6, April 1996.

5cyberconf (www.cyberconf.com)

1) info-marxism
You used the term 'lumpenproletariat', do you think that like other historical ghosts, Marxism will come back through cyberspace and free our oppressed virtual selves? How does the cybernetical info=money worldview fit together with it. Do you see an utopical option for the 'digital revolution' to overwhelm info-capitalism by bringing it to it's terminal state? With which tactics, which mantras? Or do we have just another electronic 'opium des volks', then how to break in with the material conditions...?
RU: I have no interest in bringing back any 19th century philosophers and I consider ideology to be a brain disease. I actually mean that in a literal sense. Ideology causes the brain to reject raw data that doesn't fit into the model the ideology provides for. Only by eschewing ideology and religion and really by engaging in a process of compassionate conceptual nihilism—the annihilation of concept married to an instinctive liberatory humanity—can we respond to the situation at hand. You might call it educated atavism. Having said that, one aspect of the situation at hand is that a lot of my Californian technoculture buddies subscribe to right-libertarian or anarcho-capitalist beliefs. And I do argue, as Marx did in the 19th century, that you can't have the withering away of the state until you've eliminated scarcity. Also, particularly in the late 20th century, you can't have the withering away of the state until you've built other defenses against total rape by the multinationals... but you already know this.

I believe that capitalism ultimately dissolves in the net because of infinite replicability and immateriality. It's an extraordinarily dissipative medium. Indeed, info-capitalism brings itself to its terminal state in some ultimate speed rush where all-at-onceness overwhelms the distinctions necessary to place value on money or to have exchange. When you're in at-onceness, there's no exchange involved. There's only total access and total surveillance. Of course, there's always raw physical power.

Tactically, I suggest that the young be re-seduced against the "employment ethic" here in the US. Not necessarily against work, but against pride in slavery, pride in the sale of self. So perhaps the slacker attitude should be spread. I hate slackers in my personal life. I have a terrible work ethic. I work day in and day out to defeat the work ethic and I resent people who think it's cool to be lazy and unreliable. Funny thing...

2) autonomy of cyberspace

How does the binary world model of inside and outside, mind and body, being on- or off-line work together with the idea of 'autonomy'? How can the movements of 60ies, early 80ies, early 90ies get connected to the now. In which mixes could one reach new levels of social intensity. The virtual subject which declares its own law sounds very much like what was known from art, poetry, political fights and psychosis. Should one fight for an independent cyberspace? Which territory is to defend? How to define its borders?

RU: There was a level of idealism to the demands made by radicals in the 1960s around notions of a new radical praxis, and around notions of autonomy within a kind of spontaneous collectivism, that I don't think you will ever see revived because an increasingly complexifying world culture leaves us too contaminated for absolutes. So I'm not really radical, in the purist sense. And I think we would do well to compare the situation wrought by technoculture to current and historical reality, rather than to absolute ideals. Of course, my position is ambiguous rather than oppositional. I'm oppositional towards the power configuration as it exists but not towards the notion of extreme technical revolution. There I'm ambiguously hopeful.

Anyway, I think that the binary or digital model as a kind of eschatology is so limited as to be silly—of course it's Christian... Yet it's something that we have to work with, in terms of computers, in terms of embodiment. It's one model that we have to work with for certain particular problems. It's too bad that we tend to anthropomorphize computers. I mean, that's the sort of effluvia of cyberculture that people really enjoy—changing the language, and the music, and lifestyle around fetishization of the computer as a kind of persona. I've got to admit that there's an attraction there myself. It's probably related to what historically has been a strategy of reclaiming the language and instruments of your oppression by sort of ironically embracing and aestheticising it. Although I wouldn't see it only in terms of oppression in this case, maybe oppression/liberation... although both terms are too pompous and absolute. I'm certainly convinced that embodiment is a problem. Disease is certainly a blow to autonomy, etc.

When someone declares his or her autonomy within cyberspace, I'm sure that means just don't fuckin' try to tell me what to do. Which seems to be sort of an American thing, just as our government is really moving against that kind of autonomy in the most vulgar sort of way is also an American thing. So the territory and the border to defend is the border of one's words, one's fingertips, one's actions. Don't tell me what to say. Don't tell me what to put inside my body. Don't tell me how to fuck. Very simple stuff. Of course, this is all contaminated. On a deeper level, we are told what to say by language, socialization, and there is probably some value in being aware of ourselves as biological robots. We certainly didn't invent our biology, the physical environment that we find ourselves in, the rules by which it operates.

So we generate worlds where we do make the rules. Oh, I see the next question is, in fact, about "virtual life."

3) virtual life

The life metaphor is very hip, information becomes part of a natural law, technology part of evolution, the whole technique becomes more like a pet and all kinds of Darwinisms are discussible again, one is trying to bring together machine and body — but who profits, in which interests? You are using a more wild metaphoric of life, is there a possibility to enforce a techno-vitalism in the interests of bodies, pleasure and wealth for all, or whatever model of life is the perfect one in your perspective, today?

RU: This question of vitalism is a very good one. The possibility for cyborg liberation—for an interpenetration between humans and machines, artificial life forms, nanotechnology ad infinitum—in a way that wildly expands human freedoms—to jump like a kangaroo, see like a bee, live a million years, change sexes, get ripped on drugs without physical deterioration—all of these things look possible. But what I see in front of me is not a people being vitalized and dynamic. What I see is people diligently working on the machines that will replace them. It is really a time of people being distressed and disappointed with the species while at the same time being excited and awed by the technology we've created.

In this environment, philosophies of artificial superiority like those of Minsky and Hans Moravek are gaining a lot of credence. As for who profits, well, what Arthur Kroker calls the virtual class profits from a propaganda campaign to make us see ourselves as replaceable biological units going about the great work of building the perfect artifice. The wired elite would like us to accept our superfluousness as not only natural but unimportant. That's why I remain sort of old-fashioned in clinging to a kind of vitalist romantic instinctivist core. I find something a little bit strange about the kind of post-ego, post-rave, twenty-something media gulch kids that I party with sometimes here in San Francisco. They're smart, sweet, and light. But there's no intense rebellion. And so, they're not vital.

4) the future of the future

Future is an overhyped term, do you think we will stop talking about it? what is your favorite time model at the moment? how we can avoid the redundant and self-fulfilling rhetorics of 'this is your future, adapt or die', of Zeitgeist economy, and the media policies of bundling imagination. How one could subvert a Wired future and the Net.Prawda role of this mag? Btw, what are your plans, books, projects?

RU: Future is an overhyped term. So we should be here now? I think that we would be mistaken to underestimate the speed and density of change being wrought by technical revolution. And I think that there is the sense, for anybody paying attention, that we are in motion. We're not in homeostasis. We're in process. We're molting. And that process is necessarily goal-oriented. There is—if not an end point—some point where things will suddenly be obviously different. That's very much real. Cyborgization, nanotechnology— these things have already arrived but they're also in process of intensification. As far as adapt or die goes, we need to marry the conceptual nihilism necessary for human adaptability to rapid technical change to an instinctive liberatory humanity. So we engage—rather than oppose—

this technical zeitgeist and demand that it's first goals be to make life materially better for everybody. Period. You will get a better human response to the annihilation of social and identity certainties if material uncertainty is eliminated or greatly reduced. If you follow that around the block a few times, you can come up with an argument that can engage ethologists and social Darwinists on their own terms.

5) tactics, tools and weapons

It seems that the more implicit tactics, the invisible activities, the strategic events and symbolic fights get a new potential when combined with the war machine of 'The Net'. Are counternetworks, hackers, code warriors more than a myth for the disappointed emancipatory movements and are there some examples to give? Does 'culture' function as a new kind of thing to fight for? If the state is not 'the enemy' any more but transnational corporate structure, then with which kind of knowledge, which kind of competence does one need for such fights?

RU: The myth of the hacker, the electronic guerrilla, provides a countervailing influence to the myth of total surveillance and control. The myth and the actuality of hacking, counternetworks etc. are the smallest chink in the armor of the national security state and the multinational security demi-states, but these are all, in a sense the games of boys with toys. It all kind of operates on the spy vs. spy warfare model.

But I think electronic guerrilla warfare could be effective as a kind of attention-getting, heroic, propaganda that would bring attention to a sophisticated post-scarcity, pro-freedom, compassionate political analysis if it's directed with great skill and precision. I'm not sure exactly how to get to that point.

We should be careful about strategies for "defeating" the transnational corporate structures. These things really are enormous parasitic life forms. If they die badly, they will kill off the host. So there has to be a strategy of incorporation. Former revolutionists seized the state apparatus. Despite the rush to virtuality, there's still a window of opportunity to seize the corporate structures through popular revolution, although you must realize that this will only be in the service of an agreeable compromise not some sixties vision of autonomous collectives or total economic democracy. But the structure can be attacked. Everybody sort of assumes that the structure is too amorphous and can't be attacked. I think the structures are actually less well-defended than those of the nation states and that this whole notion of invincibility through invisibility and distributed-ness of the ever mutating corporate oligarchy might be a paper tiger. For the moment.

Fleshware: Rudy Rucker Interview

Esquire Japan   Winter 1996
21•C   Spring 1996
The Day You Link to a Global Brain   Thomson Japan   Summer 1996

Novelist, scientist, iconoclast and cult hero, Rudy Rucker has emerged as a key figure in the developing technoculture, known as much for his software programming and his theories on mathematics and artificial life as for his cyberpunk Science Fiction. Rucker has published eighteen books, including the recent *Artificial Life Lab (*book with software*), Live Robots (*reissue of his two seminal cyberpunk novels, *SOFTWARE* and *WETWARE*), and *The Hacker and the Ants* (a near-future novel about artificial life in Silicon Valley). He coedited *MONDO 2000: A USER'S GUIDE TO THE NEW EDGE* with R.U. Sirius and Queen Mu. Rucker is currently teaching computer science at San Jose State University, and working on his next novel, *FREEWARE.*.

   Born in Louisville, Kentucky, in 1946, this great grandchild of Hegel received his Ph.D. in Mathematics from Rutgers University. He worked for Autodesk Inc. on their *Chaos Software* and in their Virtual Reality project.

   Rudy is laconic, funny, skeptical but not cynical. He knows as much about how the universe works as just about anybody and he's rather humble about it.

   This interview took place on his spacious sun deck on a sunny weekday afternoon, in beautiful suburban Los Altos—where else but in Silicon Valley, California.

The Mathematics of Writing and Fucking Robots

R.U. SIRIUS: You wear two hats, one as a cyberpunk science fiction writer and the other as a computer programmer and a mathematician. And your science fiction is informed by your technical and scientific knowledge. Would you say that this is pretty unique among SF writers, especially the cyberpunks?

RUDY RUCKER: Yeah, there aren't too many scientists who do fiction. There are a few. Gregory Benford, for instance, who's a physics professor. I like to do both things because it exercises different parts of my brain. I enjoy having a scientific idea and putting it into a novel. In effect, I use the novels as an experiment. I can take a scientific idea and see where it leads. Like my most recent book *The Hacker and The Ants,* I was interested in the idea of evolving robots with virtual reality. It works the other way too. A lot of the ideas I have about evolving intelligent robots, I got while writing my novels, *SOFTWARE* and *WETWARE*. I like to zigzag back and forth between fiction and technological invention.

R.U.: So things that you invent in fiction tend to come to life?

R.R.: Yeah, somewhat. I think *Hacker and The Ants* will come true in terms of people using virtual reality to evolve robots. It's really expensive to build a robot. It's cheaper to use a virtual reality model and then evolve it. But it's not like I'm Jules Verne, who wrote about submarines long before they happened. A lot of the things I write about are sort of in the air anyway.

R.U.: What are you writing now?

R.R.: *FREEWARE*. It's set in 2053. And the robots are made of plastic. (That's one of my predictions that's coming true.) Instead of being made of hard silicon chips, they're made of soft plastic. They're called Mouldies. They crawl around. They're like that morphing guy in *Terminator 2*. They can turn into a bird and fly away, or a dolphin, or a rocket ship, or a dildo. I'm putting in a lot of kinky sex.

R.U.: ...artificial living dildoes.

R.R.: Sex is usually the first thing that humans use new technologies for.

R.U.: That's the way it's frequently introduced and popularized. Do you think artificial life will be used in that way?

R.R.: Sure.

R.U.: Robots are already pretty active in industry, particularly in Japan. But maybe, in America, they will be popularized as sex toys.

R.R.: In my story there's a dildo called Dr. Jerry Falwell.

HACKING

R.U.: In *Mondo 2000's User's Guide to the New Edge,* you expressed a lot of excitement about writing software, which was something you were just starting to do at the time? Do you still feel that excitement?

R.R.: Well, as you do it more, you realize how much difficult work is involved. It takes so long to get a program to work. Still, it's a joy doing it. When I was a mathematician I could work on proofs. It's rather hard to come up with a good proof, and have it be interesting. But to get a software program that works, that you can tinker with and then actually have something, I find more satisfying. It's tactile.

R.U.: As the science of the times changes, and we work with more abstract non-physical forms, mathematicians are becoming mechanics in a sense.

R.R.: Yeah. It's a complete revolution in mathematics. It's the golden age. It's the best thing that's ever happened to me.

R.U.: Do you see yourself as an alchemist trying for the philosopher's stone?

R.R.: It's more like people are building a cathedral and I'm helping to build it. I just do this little piece.

R.U.: That's very democratic.

R.R.: That's the way hacking is. It isn't like with physics, where you might find the philosopher's stone, the secret, the little equation. With computer science, it's technical, physical. It's worldly.

I mean, if you tell people you're a mathematician they say, "I don't like math." And then there's nothing more to say. If you say you're a computer scientist, they're always full of questions: "What computer should I buy? What stocks should I get?" I like that.

CYBERPUNK

R.U.: You seem to have a slightly more optimistic take on things than most of the people who are identified with the cyberpunk genre. It's as twisty as Gibson, but it's not quite as dark.

R.R.: That's probably because Gibson's drug of choice is methedrine and mine is marijuana. Rather than being paranoid and tense, I'm euphoric... in a nutshell, that's the difference. Of course, I'm sure Bill's clean these days and so am I. (laughter) Generally, I like to be more humorous and light-hearted. I've never liked really violent stuff. Like some of the cyberpunk books, people are just constantly being blown away by the dozens. I prefer not to kill many people in my books. To me, if someone dies, it's a big deal. So I would like for there to be a reason for it. I like my characters to be important real people and not just ducks in a shooting gallery.

R.U.: Have you ever had the urge to make it really violent because it's the trendy thing to do?

R.R.: Well, now and then I do something violent—like when they cut the top of the guy's head off and eat it, I think that's sort of violent.

R.U.: Do you think the future will be more violent than the present?

R.R.: I don't know. But Cyberpunk is not so much about the future as it is about the present. And at this point in history, there's an increasing fusion of people and machines. So in my books, *SOFTWARE* and *WETWARE,* people are being turned into robots, robots into people. The boundary is blurred. And I think that we do think of ourselves as machines more than we used to. And some things from cyberpunk are coming true. The web is a fairly good model of cyberspace. If you have a Silicon Graphics machine, you can do cyberspace with a virtual reality interface.

R.U.: What about in the social realm? I always thought the idea of cyberpunk was that you would have really weird subcultures—that was the distinction from other science fiction.

R.R.: Yeah. And something that the web and the net make possible is that you can live in the Midwest where there's nobody in the particular subculture that you're into, but you have net access to a group of like-minded people.

NET LIFE

R.U.: Do you like writing on the net, talking to people and stuff like that?

R.R.: Sort of. People who find out my email address write me and I answer them. I don't join forums or anything like that.

R.U.: So you haven't delved into it as a public forum.

R.R.: Not really. Sometimes, I look at some of the newsgroups about cellular automata or about drugs or sex.

R.U.: Do you think writing online is an inspiration for a writer or a dissipation of energy?

R.R.: I think the more you write, the better you get at it. So online, you're exercising your writing ability. That sort of writing is more like conversation.

R.U.: It's somewhere in between formal writing and conversation. It's a little bit more self-conscious than conversation. You still have a brief opportunity to go back and edit yourself.

R.R.: And also there's a record of what you said. That's the risky thing about email. You do it as casually as conversation, but if you say something insulting, the person can print it out and read it over and over again. Whereas you wouldn't write somebody something as insulting in a letter, because you would look over the letter again before you send it. I've lost some friends that way. (laughter) The thing about flames is that you have to have thick skin. My most savage flames are directed at people who write to me and want to talk about Gibson's writing.

R.U.: Don't ask you about Bill, right?

R.R.: I say, why don't you go read *my* books, you stupid geek!

R.U.: You're sick of hearing about Gibson.

R.R.: Very.

R.U.: Are you interested in having your novel on the net?

R.R.: *HotWired* which is the on-line version of *Wired,* serialized an on-line novel by somebody. I don't think I'd want to publish that way because I don't think I'd be paid very much and I don't think very many people would read it. To me, the Net is *not* a good place for reading long pieces. It's not pleasant to look at the screen and it's expensive to stay online for a long time. I don't think the book will be replaced any time soon, for casual reading.

R.U.: There's a fetish for new technology going around right now, and people are willing to be very uncomfortable and deal with a really shitty medium just because it's new.

R.R.: I think it's nice. Because they're willing to do that, the medium advances. And as it advances, it gets good. I did a thing for *HotWired*. What I did was to generate a whole bunch of megabytes and make it like a hypertext collage. I cut pieces of things I've written and put those under buttons. And then I'd give away a program I've written that had something to do with the articles. People could download them. So it's a mix of text, programs, source code, pictures, and screen-captures. The net is the only place to publish something like that.

R.U.: You've been talking for years about wanting to have your entire life preserved in some kind of hypertext medium.

R.R.: Yeah, that's a prediction of mine that's coming true.

R.U.: What do you think about (Carnegie-Mellon Roboticist) Hans Moravek's notion of people actually uploading their consciousness into the net?

R.R.: I'm into it, in a way. It's a complicated question and I've thought about it alot for many years. It was sort of the idea in *SOFTWARE*—that the robots were going to get this man's personality. You would first need a database. You would need to be interrogated over a long period of time. I think that some product might be available in about ten years that would follow you around, and it would ask you questions. It would generate this hypertext file. It might be called a lifebox. You'd give it to your grandchildren and they can say "Did you ever play baseball grandpa?" and it would tell them. And they could say. "Tell me more," and so on. It will be a hypertext memoir. If it's done well enough you can actually talk to the person. Of course, just because you write your memoir, the book isn't you. You're dead. The question is, how good would the simulation have to be for you to feel like it was you?

R.U.: Or can you give it a conscious experience?

R.R.: If a robot is complicated enough, maybe it would feel like it was conscious.

R.U.: Are you an immortalist? Do you have a drive to preserve your mortal life

for as long as possible through life extension and cryonics and all that?

R.R.: No. I'm ready to go, when the time comes. I think it's stupid to want to live forever. I take the Buddhist view. There's only one mind, one consciousness. There's like a universal rain that moistens all creatures. Everything is wet with the same water, with the same consciousness. My consciousness doesn't go away when I die. It's just the cosmic consciousness and if I choose to identify with that, there's really nothing to worry about.

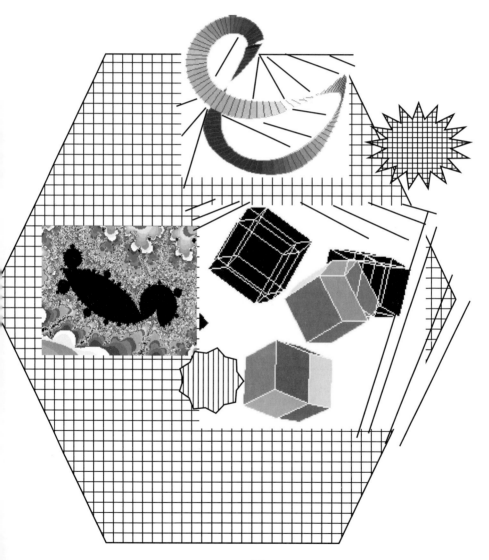

The Road Behind: Bill Gates

ARTFORUM International, April 1996

In Terry Gilliam's 1981 film *Time Bandits,* the evil overlord of the child protagonist's ever-shifting fantasy world is a slick hustler who, among other things, is hawking a high tech home of the future. The overseer leers at the young boy salaciously before launching his pitch, but the "money shot" in this gadget pornography isn't orgasm: it's domestic convenience. Convenience as the goal of 20th Century bourgeois life is one of the directors favorite themes, and it would be easy to imagine that Gilliam invented Bill Gates, CEO of Microsoft and author of the blandest book ever written about the human future, *The Road Ahead*. Gates' opus spans 286 pages in the pursuit of ever greater convenience brought to you by "friction-free capitalism"—a telling metaphor for Gates' sexless and bloodless world view.

In actuality, of course, the road ahead looks more like a disaster area. Neotribal warfare is replacing the industrial state. Various flavors of fundamentalism are pitching wildly towards millennial hysteria. We've got a handful of incipient plagues and a badly damaged ecosphere making for some strange weather. But Chairman Gates has the software that can turn your personal future into a smooth ride, where "customized information is a natural extension of the tailored consultation capabilities of the highway." This is a one-inch thick designer future written by a pinhead for pinheads. And, more to the point, *on* a pinhead capable of holding some quadrillion bits of information. It is both our fortune and our misfortune that the future, like the present, is far more novel, disordered, and horrible than this massively overpaid, prosaic engineer can even begin to apprehend, let alone give expression to.

While we have no more right to expect Gates to make a major contribution to speculative thought in the 20th Century philosophy than we would have from Henry Ford before him, in *The Road Ahead* Gates falters even within his own sphere—communications technology. His road ahead is largely the road behind.

Given his pragmatic position as a businessman/engineer, it's difficult to fault Gates for putting the same focus on the PC as a day-to-day business tool, an engine of multimedia production and a word processor, as he does on the internet. But it's exactly this sort of hardheaded engineer's gaze that causes him to get the net all wrong. He wants us to view the internet as something containable, something that exists within a discreet space provided by the PC. In fact, it's common knowledge that technological analysts have long been looking to the net to *replace* the PC as the defining medium of the age. This process should begin next year with the release of terminals used only for the Internet. As the net and the PC diverge, so will the social metaphors that have attached themselves. The PC will lose all claims of being a connecting device and will be stripped of all glamour, which dissipates anyway as any new technology becomes ubiquitous. The PC, sans net, is a lonely, asocial convenience box, naught but a complex calculator.

Bill Gates is a creature of the "PC Revolution" all the way. In fact, if you look closely, you can find a surprising degree of hostility towards the "information highway" that the book titles itself after. Using archetypically megacorporate-scale demographics, Gates invokes the internet's current, relatively small numbers (as compared to Microsoft 95 buyers, for instance?) to call into question its near future commercial viability. When he discusses the complexities of bringing net service to the level where it's convenient *(that word!)* and affordable to the average consumer, this ultimate techno-optimist suddenly becomes pessimistic, predicting a decade of laborious progress. And, finally, raising the specter of William Tappan Morris' infamous internet worm that shut down most of the net in 1988, Gates invokes the psychology of fear to separate PC isolates from net connectives. The message is that social intercourse isn't safe . You might get infected.

I don't believe that Gates' fear of the net is part of a conscious attempt by a businessman to slow a trend that could take his Microsoft out of the loop. He has, after all, shown incredible entrepreneurial flexibility and will probably find some way to keep his fingers in the internet pie. No, I think Gates just hates chaos. And the internet, bless its utterly dissipated soul, is chaos. Millions of people are chattering, uploading, downloading, linking, flirting, and—worst of all—making copies of whatever they want for free.

Among early hackers, Gates was famous for his militant stance against free software. His opponents in the hacker community pointed out the difficulty in charging money for something that was trivial to copy. Gates, of course, has become one of the richest men in the world doing just that. But his gorge rises every month as millions more log on. With everybody and their dog providing so much content and software for free, why pay for anything? Far from friction-free capitalism, the net is friction-free anarchy. It's utterly amorphous. The mind of a prosaic software engineer would dissolve in trying to wrap itself around it.

Gates doesn't even try. He evinces much more pleasure writing about his personal "home of the future," which he does at great lengths. Convenience is the mother of surveillance, and so we enter the home that Chairman Bill is currently building for himself on Mercer Island, Washington, where visitors will have a small electronic monitor pinned to their clothes. This will be connected to the smart home's CPU:

"When it's dark outside, the pin will cause a moving zone of light to accompany you through the house. Unoccupied rooms will be unlit. As you walk down a hallway, you might not notice the lights ahead of you gradually coming up to full brightness and the lights behind you fading. Music will move with you, too. It will seem to be everywhere, although, in fact, other people in the house will be hearing entirely different music or nothing at all. A movie or the news will be able to follow you around, too. If you get a phone call, only the handset nearest you will ring."

Gates' tactfully doesn't gloat over the surveillance implications here, but the message of control is as clear as it is creepy.

The world of Bill Gates is as arid as his prose. One is tempted to envision him as a communications-age Howard Hughes, attendants replaced by digital tools. But he would never be that extravagant. No, Gates is doomed to a life of bourgeois mediocrity, shining proof that the joyless Protestantism of America's old ruling class will be perpetuated by the baby-boom generation. But the rest of us should count our blessings because, with the publication of *The Road Ahead,* Gates has played his hand. And while he may be the man who sells the world, it's obvious that he hasn't a clue about what to do with it. That much will be left to the rest of us.

Timothy Francis Leary   1920 – 1996

There's nobody alive like Timothy Leary. He was literally the life of the party and now that he's gone, it feels as though the party is over. His ability to get people to have fun was unparalleled and, in its own way, mystical

HotWired, **June 1996**
MONDO **2000, 1996**

With his passing (or "de-animation," as he preferred to call it), several variations on the public Timothy Leary will be brought up for review. Leary was an extremely complex man, and he leaves behind an enormous legacy. Many legacies, in fact. Timothy himself recently said, "Everybody gets the Timothy Leary that they deserve." There are probably three primary Timothys that will pass through the public imagination over the next few years.

Leary 1 – The Acid Guru:
The primary Timothy that will pass through the mainstream media is the gleeful, irresponsible purveyor of LSD to an unsuspecting American public. Not that people who believe in this cartoon version of Timothy are necessarily *against* him. Many postmodern world citizens–from the relatively stable to the criminally insane–understand that they need to have their tight little minds royally fucked if they're ever going to have any fun, if even only for a moment.

Leary 2 – The Adventurer/Explorer:
The biographies will surely follow. For those familiar with this real-life legend of a mind, we have arguably the most poignant grail-quest/adventure story of the century: Overly optimistic transactional psychologist who believes it's possible to change the human psyche for the better stumbles upon psilocybin. He decides, "This is it!" and rushes off to tell everybody. Next thing you know, he's a figurehead for a heady moment in history when the seeming vanguard of a generation believes in a "total revolution" in human relations and consciousness. As the historic moment passes, they retreat. But Leary emerges from a series of Byzantine adventures with revolutionists, governments, prisoners, spies, and outlaws (real outlaws) still advocating novel approaches toward radically transforming the human situation, a sadder-but-wiser "hope fiend." Not so sad, however, that he didn't party like it was 1999 throughout the '80s and '90s.

Leary 3 – The Philosopher: Finally, there is the man's actual work: dozens of books, monographs, and essays. Much of his work is suffused with the cultural and political context of the moments in which it was written–a testimony to his activism. Still, Leary's essential arguments–in favor of a generous and expansive humanism, against rigid belief structures, in favor of bravely embracing novelty, against purism, in favor of levity, against gravity–are eloquent, complex, finely nuanced, and supported with observations taken from science, cultural theory, and experience.

As someone who has been profoundly affected by Leary's views, I'll take a tremendous interest in seeing how his legacy is dealt with by the media (which, with the popularization of the net, has come to mean a broad slice of the public at large). But it's the memory of Timmy as a friend that is most meaningful. And the man had so many friends. To know Tim was to love Tim. In his home, he was the world's most gracious host. Out of his home, he was *still* the world's most gracious host! He had the most infectious *joie de vivre* of anybody I've ever met. And there are a few tens of thousands of people who would agree with me.

Timothy Leary was, first and foremost, the man who brought psychedelic drugs into American culture. He was a visionary hope fiend, a libertine, an educator, an Irish drunk, a frontier scout, a tarnished hero of the '60s revolt, a highly original theorist, the genial host of the world party, a prankster, a stubborn individualist, a space cadet, a huckster, broke, a fame whore, rich, a holy fool, a well-rounded generalist with a unique ability to absorb and integrate technological and scientific materials with cultural signs and personal observations, a ladies' man, an eloquent defender of individual rights, one of the 20th century's most astute philosophers, a snake oil salesman, a sensualist, strong, brave, a *bon vivant,* weak, an underrated writer, funny, tragic, corruptible, inspiring. And the man with the highest bail in human history.

What will we do without him?

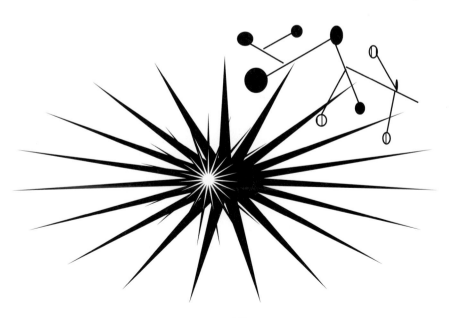

TransMutationism: An ExtroPunkian's Strange Pursuit

21•C   Summer 1996

Until the twentieth century, attempts at radically transcending biological/physical limitations in Western culture were primarily identified with the occult, and best personified by the alchemist. Mixing up mysticism, science, pseudoscience, and a batch of chemicals, the goal was nothing less than entering into a magical wish state via a magickal object. There, the problems of being human—particularly the vulnerability and aging of the physical body—was transmuted into an idealized (and beautified) state of perpetual bliss in the body. The technoscientific age pursues alchemy via the perfect hack or the magic bullet. This attempt at transcending physical limitations without dying might be labeled transmutationism.

TransMutationism reverberates across the 20th century, it's influences ranging from the woolly eugenics experiment of the occultist nazis to the pyramid-powered white magic of the new agers. In the main, however, the transmutational project has pretty much abandoned the mystical for pure science and technology. By the time we reach the 1960s, transcendence of-the-flesh in-the-flesh borders on becoming a nascent popular demand. (Witness the horror of the boomers as we age. This wasn't *supposed* to happen.) This makes perfect sense. Late 19th century abilities like flight or voice and image projection through space and time would be enough to trigger utopian hopes among primates such as ourselves. These hopes—and the inevitable companion fears—of superbeingness, were first voiced in science fiction, b-movies, and comic books, by art movements like the Futurists and, politically, almost exclusively by the fascists. In the 1960s, transmutationism appears as a modest undertow in the countercultural and libertarian movements (largely owing to psychedelic and science fictional influences). Finally, transmutationism emerges as a fully conscious and, some would say, realistic element of the technoculture trope of the nineties. Augmented, cyborged, or post-biological, the mutant human surfaces occasionally or implicitly in the upbeat *Wired*/corporate version of technoculture, and is explicitly envisioned in the more ambiguous cyberpunk version.

Under the influence of the silicon chip, biotech, artificial life, space exploration, biological computing, the hope of nanotechnology, the Hubble telescope, advanced medical techniques, advances in gerontology, designer drugs, and virtuality, we now have among us an apparent new species, superhumanity's "early adopters." The nascent wish for transcending the troubling limitations of the meat has long been surpassed by a near hysterical impatience with its limitations. With all of this technical magic and hyperreality at our fingertips, the primate wonders, why must this ridiculous slab of flesh still suffer?

On the political level, this impatience with physical existence has found its expression in the unexpected revolt of the transmutating privileged against the ordinary—non-transcended humans. It manifests as the politics of abandonment advocated by the technolibertarians and informs the current Republican sponsored war against the impoverished in America.

So it's not surprising that Ayn Rand's objectivist philosophy would form the ideological foundation for the best known organized group of superhuman, or postbiological, early adopters. The Extropy Institute (extropy means the opposite of entropy) sports a fine technovisionary pedigree. Included among its members are Marvin Minsky, nanotechnology mainman Eric Drexler, and Hans Moravek, the Carnegie-Mellon based roboticist best known for his advocacy of downloading human consciousness onto silicon. When I attended their annual "Extropian Convention" last year in Sunnyvale, California, I was appalled by the dominance of discourse about market ideology over technological innovation.

True Extropunkian TransMutationist Grit

OK. This is where I have to come out of the closet. Think of me as an Extropunkian. I'm out to democratize obscene and scary Godlike powers. My own politics of desire forces me somewhere within the same framework as these thin-lipped *Fountainhead*-waving whiteboys. I *want* long distance viewing, replaceable body parts, memory chips, a nanotechnology-based leisure lifestyle of infinite wealth, an anti-aging pill, and the perfect aphrodisiac. I *want* the technology that's indistinguishable from magic even to those people already familiar with that Arthur C. Clark quote. I mean, when they say, "Lookie here, Chucko. This is the choice. You can die a slow, dreary, and painful death from cancer or you can take this here pill, reverse the aging process, be smart as a whip, fuck four times a day and eat fried pig guts right before bed and not get gas," — what say *you?*

Of course, this battle to define the terms of superhumanity is bracketed by failure. All of our technological reality hacks seem to have their costs. Things break down. Artificial organs malfunction. The Biosphere II loses its oxygen supply. Smart drugs cause ulcers... things... break... down. As Bruce Sterling told *MONDO 2000*, "...if you could become a cyborg for reasons of intellectual ecstasy, one day you'd discover that you'd passed out in the street and there are roaches living in your artificial arm."

Failure. Which only goes to prove that the techno-utopians, the extropians, the digital early adapters and even your humble extropunkian commentator are propelled not by objectivism but by the ancient and ridiculous—but undeniably romantic—quest for the philosopher's stone, the holy grail, and all that. Hey. As my friend Zarkov once said, "It beats bowling."

What About Cyberdelia?
R.U. Sirius vs. Mark Dery

Mark Dery is a brilliant writer, but he insists on seeing people as little boxes of ideology. And if you say something once, Dery will be holding you to it a decade later. Literally. But I like Mark. When Hotwired *asked me who I would like to go up against in their public debate section that they named "Brain Tennis," I foolishly chose to debate Dery about "Cyberdelia." Foolish because I was choosing to make an argument for something I feel very ambiguous about—utopianism. In fact, I'm not a utopian. Not only don't I believe in perfection, I find the notion scary. But I guess I'm an approximate utopian. Kevin Kelly and the high guard at* Wired *were quite enthusiastic about how I carried this off. Should I be proud or shamed?*

Hotwired **October 16, 1996**

Wired:

Could the cyberdelic "utopian" culture represented by *Mondo 2000* and Timothy Leary (among others) have anything positive to offer to the information culture of the 1990s, or is it just a variation on the washed-up '60s fantasy of getting high and "dropping out"?

R. U. Sirius, a writer, prankster, iconoclast, unapologetic psychonaut and co-founder of *Mondo 2000,* claims we need to work less and play more. His most recent book is *How to Mutate & Take Over the World: An Exploded Post-Novel.*

Mark Dery, a cultural critic, author of *Escape Velocity: Cyberculture at the End of the Century,* a critique of fringe computer culture and editor of the essay collection *Flame Wars: The Discourse of Cyberculture,* says R. U. and other *Mondo*-ites are "insulated from the grimmer social realities inside their high-tech comfort zones.

1
R.U. Sirius

Caveat: please note that "utopianism" is in quotes. We're dealing with an approxima-tion here. Having said that...

Any movement away from dwindling hopes, freedom rendered moot by fear, and the slow murder of the underclass will be energized by a psychedelic "utopian" pres-ence. Further, we could end scarcity while vastly increasing personal autonomy dur-ing the coming decade. In that sense, psychedelic "utopianism" is even realistic.

Sade said, "What's the point of a revolution without general copulation?" That goes double for a digital Revolution. Are we here to build a vast cosmic accounting system or to have a kickass fucking party while the machines do the work? Soberly, you'll say neither. But I'll let the world's most powerful Clinton... George...

set the terms of my discourse. He said, "Free your mind and your ass will follow." I agree. Oops. Looks like I've exceeded the age of reason here.

Let's fuck with the mind first, since the cultural superego (involved in boundary maintenance) is the first line of defense for the *ancien régime.* Passive acquiescence to mainstream politics (consensus reality) functions by the maintenance of constrict sing illusions, false boundaries. For instance, an obsolete and capricious definition of value (money) sentences us all to original debt. Taboos render public discourse dishonest. Etcetera.

Surrealism, drugs, paganism, sexual libertinism, the Dionysion impulse in rock culture, subcultural anarchism, all are attempts to storm the Bastille of the cultural superego... the controlling forebrain, liberate aspects of the libido, id, and ego—and experience agape or ecstasis. (Incidentally, these are matters of experience, not belief.)

Mirroring this process across the 20th Century, the dispersion of media/communications technology—sold to us by the corporate oligarchy—has provided former yokels access to deviant minds, and digital media has decentralized attention. This has accelerated and amplified the assault on cultural boundaries, dissipating consensus reality and overwhelming fixed identity.

And now, your ass will follow. Because work, i.e. employment or wage slavery, is obsolete. The solid, secure, agricultural/industrial era, production-oriented forms of labor have been displaced by automation and dissipated by the global work force. There has never before been a time in history where a majority of people have been forced to hustle so pointlessly, toiling the fields of hype, poisoning the real and conceptual environment with bogus product, desperately servicing invented needs, building massive unnecessary arsenals, clearcutting the forests etc.

This is, of course, all problematized by a well-armed, multinational corporate oligarchy that won't share the wealth, a still solid core of fear and reaction among the masses, and your own trendy cynicism. But the first completely digital generation—our nation's teens—are online, on drugs, and ready to riot. My work here is nearly done.

2

Mark Dery

The *political* usefulness of cyberdelic utopianism — what-me -worry Futurism confected from '60s romanticism, '90s cyberculture, the menopausal mysticism of the millenarian New Age, and the apolitical self-absorption of the human potential movement — is dubious at best.

Your rehabilitation of the Dionysian wing of the counterculture consists of retrofitting Yippie visions of a post-scarcity Paradise Now of endless leisure, all watched over by machines of loving grace, for the 21st century. Wet(ware) dreams of having a "kickass fucking party while the machines do the work" aren't new, of course: Arthur C. Clarke imagined an "uninhibited, hedonistic society" of cradle-to-grave leisure, made possible by "ultraintelligent" machines, in a 1968 *Playboy*.

Few would deny the unhappy fact of artificial scarcity, cynically manufactured by political opportunists, or the feasibility of ending, say, world hunger, if multinational agribusiness were to link arms with Sally Strutters. Nor would many dispute the no-brainer that work sucks.

But your post begs the obvious: What's in it for Archer Daniels Midland? How can the transnational corporate monoliths, and the lapdog nation-states whose legislation is increasingly written by their lobbyists be cajoled or compelled into granting what you've elsewhere called "an unconditional, livable, guaranteed annual income to all human beings?" And how is "general copulation" going to bring the Great Moloch to its knees and usher in your ludic, libertarian paradise?

You can't build a revolution on the pleasure principle. Cyberdelic utopianism's most pernicious dynamic is that it skins countercultural style and leaves the '60s political guts — the civil rights movement, emergent feminism, the very notion of activist politics — behind. The hippie article of faith that "drugs, paganism," and the like will cure society's ills by unchaining the id and dethroning the repressive "cultural superego," thereby returning us to the Garden of Earthly Delights, is beer-bong mysticism of the most dangerously naive sort.

It is essentially *psychological,* rather than *political,* in nature, and springs from the brow of the Freudian psychologist Norman O. Brown, a '60s prophet of "polymorphous perversity" you're fond of invoking.

The obvious problem with a psycho-politics based on "ecstasis" is that it circles its wagons around the individual psyche while ceding the real world (a particularly worrying tendency given the secession from the social sphere epitomized by the private, gated enclaves that are the fastest-growing residential communities in the U.S.). At a time when democracy is profoundly imperiled by corporate influence-peddling, public disaffection with the political process, and the ever-widening chasm between the economic elite and the downsized masses, taking refuge in retro-hippie fantasies of what you've called a "new society governed by eros" is the political equivalent of a fractal screensaver.

3

R.U. Sirius

First... the next culture critic that calls me new age, I tear out its nosering with my teeth. Slapping labels and presumptive ideologies on everybody may impress the theory rubes, but it only *diminishes* insight. We *burned down banks* in the 60s, OK?!! I didn't see Shirley McLaine around. I *hate* insipid new age philosophy. I quoted Sade, not Rajneesh. Talk to *me!*

Unfortunately most people do *not* agree that scarcity is false or that the work ethic "sucks." If they perceived a substantial distinction between what is and what could be, they would be more inclined towards revolution.

Techno-yippieism is about spreading post-scarcity consciousness. That was premature in the sixties. In the digital age, it's *necessary.* Automation and globalization are rendering most people economically superfluous. *Already* over 50% of Americans are unemployable, unemployed, working temp, or without benefits or job security. Work is on its way out. The only alternative to a world of serfs and slaves abandoned by a self-sufficient corporate oligarchy is a rabble revolution of slackers, rising up to demand the fruits of the technology that has displaced them. "Free your mind and your ass will follow" guided my initial discourse. The reverse is also true.

How's the left doing these days, Mark? When was the last time it was on the rise, when it captured the energy of rebellious youth? What else was going on at the time? Maybe a psychedelic, cultural and sexual revolution?

Listen. We get all button-down, hyper-rational, and righteous when we talk political solutions. Deep down, we know it's horseshit. Libidinally speaking, we don't even *want* to make nice. The genius of the hip left sixties was that it resolved that tension by enclosing the erotic, the atavistic, the visionary—within a philosophy of humanism, unifying the personal and political, desire and altruism, under an ideal of liberation. Embracing pleasure — resisting puritanism and mental rigidity — energizes any revolt against political oppression, *particularly* in a post-labor world. *That* should be a no-brainer.

But let me turn this around. You accuse me of dwelling on the psychological. Do you deny us an interior life? You dismiss freeing the unconscious and the ecstatic. Do you prefer bourgeois propriety? You dis polymorphous perversity. Do you prefer monomorphic single-mindedness?

Probably we're both losers. The changes either of us want won't happen. At least I'm encouraging people to have a good time. What about you? I think your brain cells could use a carnival blast. You know, when you come to the end of your quest for highbrow intellectual credibility, you'll discover only one thing: Rigor is a condition of death.

4

Mark Dery
I'd say the adjective "New Age" was adequately earned by a subcultural phenomenon (cyberdelic utopianism) whose house organ *(Mondo)* showcased John Lilly holding forth on being "zapped" by a "blast of telepathic information" from one of his cetacean psychic friends.

Let's return to the *ideas* at hand, shall we? I need no convincing on the point that "work is on its way out," although you neglect to mention that the world of post-industrial sweetness and light is made possible not only by automation but by the relocation of manufacturing, thanks to NAFTA and GATT, to what is quaintly called "the developing world."

But my question about how transnational corporate power and their toady nation-states could be coaxed or compelled into creating your *Jetson*ian welfare state on DMT hangs in the air, unanswered. Apparently, we're supposed to commend our hopes to a "revolution of slackers," a spontaneous uprising of the BarcaLounger brigade. This word "Revolution," which fellow '60s traveler Louis Rossetto is equally fond of, is nervous-making; it exudes the hubris of the true believer confident that history has a telos, and it's going his way. How's the left these days, R.U.? Alive and well, judging by the delicious irony that libertarian digerati and cyberdelic utopians alike seem to embrace Marx's technology worship and his born-again conviction that the Revolution will usher in a workers' paradise made possible by automation.
By the way, your jaw-dropping assertion that "the hip left" of the '60s "resolved the tension" between "desire and altruism" shreds historical fact. "There were tensions galore" between the New Left and the bohemian "freaks," writes Todd Gitlin in *The Sixties.* "Radicalism's tradition [was] Marx: change the world! The counterculture — Leary, the Pranksters — were descended from Emerson, Thoreau, Rimbaud: change consciousness, change life!"

We'll ring down the curtain of mercy on the rest of your argument, which descends into apoplectic ad hominem about my "brain cells requiring a carnival blast" — a Furry Freak Brother's last recourse, in a losing battle. *Of course* I'm not denying the value of "the unconscious and the ecstatic" (although "polymorphous perversity" has always struck me as a figment of the overheated Freudian imagination), R.U.; I'm debating the notion that those ideas can be the cornerstones of a pragmatic politics, a concept that would make a cow laugh. And as for the anti-intellectual bilge that we all know, "deep down," that "political solutions" are "horseshit," this is precisely the sort of wisdom one would expect from a disciple of Norman O. Brown, who held that "the loins are the place of judgment" — a not entirely untrue assertion, at least in this instance.

5

R.U. Sirius

Mark, I was closer to the new lefties than the dropouts in the sixties. Psychedelic drugs, sexual freedom, artistic experimentation, philosophic openness, a sense of pranksterish fun: all these things were ubiquitous. They were part of the zeitgeist.

You ask "how transnational corporate power and their toady nation-states could be coaxed or compelled into creating" (or allowing) a post-scarcity economy that sets the wage slaves free. I offer no blueprint.

I only know that it will *not* happen if nobody advocates it. And I know that exponential technological growth — probably culminating with self-replicating production technologies — replaces workers. And I know that if you don't reorient society towards allowing "employment" to end, we'll see ugly, desperate suffering amidst astounding wealth. And I know that cutting edge capitalism is now in a pure transacting economy of derivatives, currency exchanges, options etc. with little reference to usable human wealth. And so, I know that the society can survive a relatively small number of people conjuring vast fortunes by the manipulation of money as information. And I know that since money is now an amorphous, redefinable process—the debt and deficit are bogus. So I suspect that we're *already* in a post-scarcity situation.

Call me Pollyanna, but for some crazy reason I think getting some young, pre-socialized (unbrainwashed) people to comprehend that the world of poverty and debt they're inheriting is a scam might just motivate them towards activism. From my experience, most people are well-defended against these types of ideas. I can't imagine why, but the ability to grasp an end to scarcity and most forms of alienated labor in a flexible, generous, pluralistic economic and political system seems inversely related to the tightness of a person's asshole. That's one reason why I advocate mental, cultural and sexual lubrication.

I don't know exactly how the corporate oligarchy can be changed or overturned. I don't know exactly how we would transition into a post-scarcity society if the general political will was to do it. I offer no cornerstones. I am the least fanatical advocate of extreme ideas you'll ever meet. It took us months to agree on this topic because I wanted to qualify everything with almosts, possiblies, and maybes. I never said that liberation of the unconscious, or raving till dawn, would magically transform the world, hundredth monkey-like. I offer a reasonably self-consistent argument that psychedelic "utopianism" conflates rather nicely with the situation wrought by technolgy that change is motivated by hope, and that flexible minds make change happen. The blueprint will have to wait until more people grasp the basic possibilities.

6

Mark Dery

Since cyberdelic utopianism turns on a selective memory of the '60s, I'm going to worry my point — namely, that you elide the profound disjuncture between switched-on bohemianism and political radicalism — with pit-bull doggedness.

By "new lefties," I presume you mean the Diggers, whose vision of a post-scarcity anarchist arcadia made possible by automation seems to be keystone of your erotic politics. But the Diggers were Marxists in the *Duck Soup* sense only, as Gitlin argues in his hilarious account of their logic-bombing of the SDS's 1967 conference, which he calls a "comic collision" between the SDS's "sobersided" political radicals and the Diggers' electric Kool-Aid brigades.

Following Norman O. Brown, you suture the philosophical rupture between the political and personal — change-the-world! versus change consciousness! — by means of a Brownian motion (forgive pun) that diagnoses societal ills in Freudian terms, reducing the social sphere to a mass psyche whose "cultural superego" needs a megadose of Turbo-Lax. Hence, the prescription of the loosened sphincter and the sexual Jiffy Lube as cultural cure-alls, updated with a Leary-esque faith in high-tech deus ex machinas. (Leary bequeathed to pop culture the uniquely American notion that the key to cosmic consciousness and sweeping social change could be packed into a capsule).

But if getting in touch with our anal-expulsive inner children were the key, wouldn't Howard Stern have freed us already? And shouldn't we be wary of political appeals to the id and the libido, given the inauspicious example of the Third Reich, whose disastrously effective stagecraft relied on Wagnerian mysticism and an ersatz Teutonic "paganism" to bypass critical resistance in its manipulations of the public mind?

I see you've dodged my point that not all limits are artificially imposed from above, which I suppose the ace-in-the-hole of "self-replicating production technologies" (codeword: nanotechnology) allows you to do. But visions of endless leisure and infinite abundance driven by Drexler's engines of change are a long shot at best, and the ticking time bomb of middle- and lower- class unrest and immiseration can't wait. While (arguably) theoretically possible, nanotech has yet to produce a single product, and thus remains pure vaporware — a sci-fi upgrade of alchemy's Universal Solvent. If its promise isn't realized, *someone* in your anarchist technotopia is still going to have to work in the old-fashioned, rust-belt sense of the word; software requires hardware. Alternatively, if nanotech arrives on schedule, it will be brought to you by corporate capitalism, whose record of environmental responsibility and social consciousness inspires Ballard-ian visions of the Bhopal disaster in one's bloodstream. Who's going to manufacture these alchemical engines, anyway? Dow-Corning

7

R.U. Sirius

Mark Dery's been arguing against an absolutist utopian follower of an obscure post-Freudian psychologist who believes that combining fabulous orgasms with strong drugs and great technology will lead to *endless* leisure and *infinite* abundance. Perhaps some day he'll debate *me*.

Forgetting Dery, I'll review the memes I've attempted to ejaculate into the body politic:

1) Technology is replacing workers. The alternative to killing off the superfluous mass of humanity lies in increased leisure. Here's an exercise. Think of all the things that people do to make a living: wrapping Hostess Twinkies, selling crack, doing pr for Hulk Hogan, building obsolete nukes, debating Mark Dery. How many people do you know who are engaged in making a bigger contribution than the average welfare mom?

2) The worldwide process by which the international financial community is tightening its belt around the throat of the indebted poor while fattening themselves masks a continuous increase in *actual* wealth. Actual wealth corresponds to humanity's knowledge and technological abilities to make use of resources.

3) Vision and pleasure are good. Progressive movements flower when people are motivated by self-interest to resolve collective problems — because their lives could be better. Conversely, the deep puritanical assumption that the good is accomplished by saintly self-denial is a lie.

What I'm *not* saying:

1) All activities will suddenly cease. The world will be a psychedelic butterscotch sunshine daydream full of beautiful people.

2) It's easy. Making change is easy. Since there's a technological, macroeconomic shift towards post-scarcity and leisure, there'll be no difficulties, no complexities, no

3) There's *only* pleasure. There's no pain. You can consume as much dope as you can fit in your veins and fuck monkeys while you dance naked amidst the deregulated biotech organisms.

I don't expect to close the sale on a series of probably unfamiliar propositions in 1800 words. The evidence every day in the real world is that we're about as close to a "psychedelic utopia" as I am to winning the Presidential election. I only hope that I've opened the discourse and piqued the reader's curiosity.

Now, Mr. Dery... I think I've figured out what a culture critic does. (S)he rummages through your work, isolating words, ideas, and phrases. (S)he removes all contexts, complexifying resonances, qualifiers, and indications of intentional, playful extravagance. She ignores all other materials that might contradict the isolated content around which (s)he builds an analysis. (S)he unilaterally slaps her own meaning on the quarantined content, pins it to the operating table and pronounces on it, being careful not to absorb any new data. Case closed

8
Mark Dery
I find your kvetchings and cavilings about my supposed refusal to "debate you" passing strange, given my point-by-point responses to your posts. And your *petit mal* seizure about "culture critics" is unintentionally hilarious. Perhaps these outbursts are the "liberation of the id," red in tooth and claw, called for in your first post.

In any event, it bears pointing out, since you seem to think I've reduced you to a straw man, that my arguments are solidly sandbagged with quotes from your posts or recent essays. If you bristle at being typed a "utopian follower of an obscure post-Freudian psychologist" (your words), then it would behoove you to distance yourself from Norman O. Brown-ian visions of a society "governed by eros," whatever that means (*ARTFORUM,* February 1996). Hand your opponent a monogrammed petard, and he'll happily hoist you by it.

As for your memetic ejaculate (which I'll observe biohazard bunny-suit protocol in handling), I take your repeated point — (familiar from Robert Reich's *Work of Nations* — that automation is displacing workers and that it lies within the high-tech West's power to provide at least the bare necessities of existence to its downsized masses. I still don't understand how we're going to get from here to there, given the monolithic roadblocks of transnational capitalism and the nation-state, or who's going to operate the machinery while the rest of us loaf contentedly. Nor do I place much stock in a post-scarcity technotopia brought to us by a "rabble revolution of slackers" and "self-replicating production technologies." But I have no quibble, in principle, with your proposition that the post-industrial state would be wiser to subsidize the leisure of the dislocated and the de-skilled than to consign them to the minimum-wage dustbin of history, to grow restless and rebellious. (Although I can't help wondering how long it would be before all that endless leisure began to weigh heavily on them, becoming a more unbearable servitude, in time, than the service-sector purgatory of yore.)

But we began with the question of whether "cyberdelic 'utopian' culture" had anything to offer the information age, and I'd like to end by reasserting that its political usefulness is next to nil. The only "cyberdelic" element here has been the mothballed theory of mass psychology, exhumed from the '60s, that underwrites your romantic vision of human nature as raw, throbbing libido repressed by "button-down hyper-rationality" — a roach-clip Freudianism now thoroughly discredited. Though it may come to you by way of the Diggers, your vision of a worker's paradise enabled by automation is textbook Marx in all the essentials — a sweet irony that would gladden the heart of the old German devil.

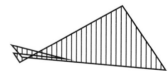

Mark Dery (markdery@well.com, http://www.levity.com) is a cultural critic. He wrote "Escape Velocity: Cyberculture at the End of the Century" (Grove Press, 1996) and edited "Flame Wars: The Discourse of Cyberculture" (Duke University Press, 1995). His essay on media activism and guerrilla information warfare, "Culture Jamming: Hacking, Slashing, and Sniping in the Empire of the Signs," is endlessly recirculated on the Internet. His collection of essays, "The Pyrotechnic Insanitarium: American Culture on the Brink," was published by Grove Press in Feburary, 1999.

Empathy For the She-Devil R.U. (hearts) Courtney

MIGHT, Winter 1996-1997

Every emotion has been utterly commodified. This is, of course, a banal truism. Something that wouldn't be banal would be if, instead of you reading my words in *MIGHT* magazine, I was gouging your left eye out with a pointed stick. Then we could confront the reality that somebody else's rage CAN have an impact on you. It would be difficult to be smug and smirkingly genx cool if I were gouging out your left eye with a pointed stick. You must admit this.

Occasionally, rock and roll at least expresses the *will* to gouge your left eye out with a pointed stick. Sometimes, it's inartful (G.G. Allin). But when it has poetry in its soul, it makes me feel less alone. When Courtney Love says that she wants to "IMPLODE right under the signed pic of Doris Day. Hey boy, i'll show you a black hole, Mr. Hawking..." on AOL, that's good enough for me. Combine that with the passion of *Live Through This* and her many other high profile acts of public disturbance and—as far as I'm concerned, she's *allowed*. She gets to play sacred monster. She can kill her next two wives if she wants, just like Jerry Lee Lewis. She has my support. Don't be denied, Courtney.

Now, consider Sid Vicious, moron and lady killer. You could have fit his entire brain into one of Courtney's neurons and still had room left over for Nancy's. And yet Sid is somehow remembered with a kind of fondness. He's the bad boy who carried that rock and roll destructo energy to its logical extreme.

Little Richard said that rock and roll has to be hot or cold, never lukewarm. In these days of flaccid and whiny self-conscious genx rockers, the only major figure who REALLY runs hot is Courtney. If she were a boy, she'd be understood in a long line of rock Dionysian assassins from Jerry Lee Lewis to Jim Morrison to the aforementoned Sid. But despite a seeming cultural hunger for bad grrrl examples, we only permit bad boys to be our sacred monsters.

Of course, *Live Through This* couldn't be denied. But the work she's doing preserving the fine rock tradition of excess in the pretend-hip decade of the tight asshole is—to put it mildly—underappreciated.

In fact, because she only gets to approximate the emotion of gouging your eye out with a pointed stick, and because she's a chick in a baby doll dress, you get to smirk with impunity. But what if I ripped out your nosering with my teeth?

We Are Duchampians of the World

World Art, **January 1997**

Duchamp's "Fountain" pissed a lot of people off. It was a frivolous gesture, turning a urinal upside-down, signing it "R. Mutt" and maintaining the fiction that it had been sent in to the open 1917 French exhibition (which refused to display it) by somebody from Philadelphia. It was a spontaneous act, one that Duchamp attached little importance to. It was a raspberry toward the very notion of art as special.

It was not the first of Duchamp's readymades, although it was the first pure readymade, recontextualizing a single artifact without change, other than the signature. And it's the one that has resonated down through art history. Ironically, for Duchamp, gestures like "Fountain" were attempts to silence that narrative (art history). As Robert Motherwell said, "Marcel Duchamp did not want to impose a new revolutionary language, but to propose an attitude of mind." He was stripping the aesthete bare, asking art consumers to experience without explanation, analyses, or retinal judgment or appreciation.

Duchamp maintained his philosophic autonomy from the art historical narrative by observing repeatedly that this history itself is subjective and accidental. It's a terribly obvious point and yet one that Duchamp alone emphasized. Interviewed by Pierre Cabanne shortly before his death, Duchamp said "... the history of art is what remains of an epoch... but it's not necessarily the best of that epoch... it's probably an expression of the mediocrity of the epoch, because the beautiful things have disappeared—the public didn't want to keep them." His utter disbelief in the notion of masters is expressed in the same interview, "I don't have a sort of... astonishment, or curiosity... Never, I'm talking about the old masters... I was really defrocked, in the religious sense of the word... All that disgusted me."

PRANKS FOR THE MEMORIES

Oddly, while Duchamp maintained no interest in the trajectory of history, he frequently stated that his work was for posterity. Was he possessed of some sort of prescience, knowing that his signal (with Fountain as the main signifier) would be picked up by postmoderns at the turn of the century, and that Duchampian themes of appropriation, recontextualization, pranking, identity hacking, and humorous self-deflation, would become part of a large-scale slacker refusal? It's doubtful. His statements against repetition would appear to exclude any other participants from Duchampianism. "Repeat the same thing often enough and it becomes taste... the enemy of art."

It's not an easy conundrum for us to sort out. Transgression has, in fact, become a familiar language. It has become aestheticized as gesture and, to some degree, trivialized as prank. If there isn't already a web site dedicated to reviewing and rating the aesthetic quality of transgressive acts done in the name of art, there certainly will be.

Familiarity breeds contempt. And familiarity with transgressive experimentation as a strategy of an artistic subcultural refusal renders it impotent. The hip, sophisticated nineties bourgeois is well-defended. The smug "been there done that" dismissal would appear to ensure that the modern equivalent of Fountain will not register as more than a passing consumer fancy for a predictable underground. Jeff Koons actually deserves some credit for his attempt at marrying Duchampian themes of puckish recontextualization to bourgeois conservatism. His "Ushering In Banality" exhibit was, at least, the first attempt since Warhol to escape from the familiar oppositional clichés of the avant-garde.

Duchamp once said that "a painting that does not shock isn't worth painting"— a statement that actually says, "Painting isn't worth it." He, of course, left painting behind. Eventually, he left the readymades behind as well, after they lost the capacity to surprise. Today, the only way one would shock a reasonably sophisticated citizen of urban America would be by delivering the right quantity of electrical current to said person's body. What would Duchamp have done in this afternoon of the living dead? My guess is — nothing. Marcel probably would have been a true slacker. After all, he said "... I'm enormously lazy. I like living, breathing, better than working." In this sense, the average person, responding from the point of view of the work culture, who would see in Fountain a case of the artist "getting away with" not having to work, is probably closer to the mark than the art historian who attempts to aestheticize it as a sort of found Brancusi.

It's the End of the Art World as we Know it and I Feel Fine

At a moment where many believe that aesthetics are the ethics of the future, Fountain can still be read as an attempt to remove aesthetics from consideration. Instead of aesthetics, it provides a slackerly invitation to relax and play without concern for reputation, history, competition, or labor. Considered in that way, Fountain's statement, once understood need never be repeated. It says today exactly what it said at its inception:

stop

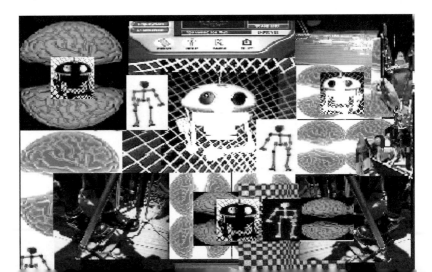

Why I'm REVOLTING!

REVOLTING! is such a great idea. A radical tabloid for Generation X. It's so fucking obvious that doing this as a print periodical... say bi-weekly on National Enquirer *type newsprint for distribution in the hipper urban and college communities would be an enormous hit—that it's shameful that no venture capitalist has come forward to say "Let's do it." But that's why I'm still revolting.*

I did one issue, online. I got what I believe is the last interview with Charlie Manson extant. Well, the interview—conducted by Richard Metzger—was actually with Manson's webmaster, George Stinson. But Stinson forwarded a couple of questions to Manson and Chuck answered them. Perfect Manson, too. Sometimes brilliant. Sometimes stupid. Sometimes enlightened. Sometimes scary. We got this nasty picture of Charlie sticking his tongue out at the camera. Manson as psycho-prankster. We put it on our front page along with 26 unsolicited rotating banner ads for various corporate entities like AOL and Microsoft. We got some great press, and only a handful of cease and desist letters. When we got the letters, we ceased and desisted. After a couple of months, we replaced all the banner ads with a parody of ABC's self-deprecating ad campaign. The initial issue also included a gateway where we violated Wired *magazines copyright on the term "Digital Revolution" and Radio Shack's claim to sole usage of the word "Shack" in a title. It said, "WELCOME TO REVOLTINGSHACK. HOME OF THE DIGITAL REVOLUTION." Never heard from those corporate lawyers either.*

I hope that someday REVOLTING! reaches its full potential. On that day, it'll be a new motherfucking dawn indeed.

Editorial by R.U. Sirius, REVOLTING!, April 1997
WHY I'M REVOLTING!

Sometimes I think that maybe I should just get smug. The newspapers are trumpeting the good news—the economy is up, crime is down, consumer confidence is high. Of course, a few million people are suddenly finding it hard to breath (link to report on asthma), but what the fuck—maybe this New World Order is the best of all possible worlds, given the complexity of our eight billion strong civilization.

So why is it that, at least once a day, I feel like climbing on top of a tall building (preferably on Wall Street) and unleashing a fusillade? Is it just a personal failing? Maybe so. Now, maybe you know who R.U. Sirius is. Maybe you don't. But, along with Queen Mu, I was the first goddamned person to use the terms "cyberculture" and 'the new edge." Yup. I'm responsible for some of that horseshit that my dear friend John Perry Barlow gets $100,000 per second to spew. (Maybe it's not horseshit. Recently, I commented to John, "this cyberstuff is pretty much horseshit isn't it?" I thought I was taking co-responsibility for some of the most banal hype of the nineties. But he disagreed. John is earnest, to say the least. I love JPB, if you don't know..)

My (our) *MONDO 2000* led to the excrescence of *Wired*. Smug little whitebread motherfucking toy-fetishizing overfed cunts (and I'm referring almost exclusively to Caucasoid males) all over the world now get to think of themselves as the hippest of the hip. *I* did that. OK... I didn't do it alone.

Umm, that's debatable actually. You know what I *hate* more than anything else? People who can't hang with psychotic megalomaniac ambiguously humorous lust-filled fuck-all beyond-the-pale hangloose drugged-up revolting people. And people who think that a joke is only a joke. In fact, any time anybody says, "Oh that's *just*"... BANG! Fist in the face. Nothing is ever *just* anything.

Our Mission
Our mission at REVOLTING! is to drive a virtual rented truck filled with 4,000 pound of homemade explosives right up the tight little trademarked, lawyer-infested, well-oiled (with money) sphincter of old and new media culture and splatter it to Queendom come.

Why do I want to do that? Because mediocre fuckfaces like Michael Ovitz make hundreds of millions of dollars and get to run dynamic businesses that achieve their aims, those aims being putting out stupid, distracting movies, each one of which costs more money than certain entire African countries filled with hundreds of thousands of starving children, while *I* have to struggle to pay my rent.

Ultimately, that's why I'm REVOLTING! I've been out here on the periphery of media culture for the entire decade, pointlessly jumping through hoops, almost scoring deals from various entertainment, technocultural, and publishing entities. I've listened to what both the foot soldiers and the powerhouses in the world of communitainment think makes a project worth doing and not worth doing. And believe me, these people need to be shot. With ketamine at the very least. "R.U., we love ya baby, but we think this just isn't a commercial enough idea for us. Maybe you could borrow $50 from your mommy and live in your car for another five years and..." BOOM! Out goes a kneecap.

REVOLTING! Guerrillas? No. That Would Be Wrong
Don't get me wrong. I'm not a violent person... most days. But I would like to gently suggest that the only solution to the current problem of lopsided access to resources unmatched since the days when we actually called nobles and serfs what they are is for a team of independent assassins to kill all the billionaires.

Calm down. This ain't exactly Pol Pot. One could still keep up to $999.999,999.99. It simply seems to me that a certain balance needs to be restored to the human economic. I simply can't believe that Bill Gates is a more valuable human being than all of the school teachers in America combined. Even if you doubt the existence of "justice" (and I do), there comes a time when things get too out-of-balance and needs to be corrected.

Getting the government to tax all income beyond a billion won't work. Too many loopholes on the one hand and more bureaucracy on the other. Anyway, it's *their* government. No. The best approach is to let the word go out, internationally, that it's too dangerous to have *that* much money.

Now, I'm not suggesting that REVOLTING! cadre meet in secret locations in the Bavarian Alps on May 1 in the year 1998 to enjoy good beer and a retinue of blonde-haired blue-eyed sex slaves of all nine genders paid for by Moammar Khadafy and plot out the beginnings of this world-wide revolt. No. And please don't do any radical deeds in my name, thus bringing unwanted controversy that might draw attention to all the books, recordings, lecture tours, and periodicals I'm trying to sell. That would be wrong. In fact, forget everything I've just said.

RADICAL TABLOIDISM: A **REVOLTING!** IDEOLOGY FOR **REVOLTING!** TIMES

Say what thou wilt shall be the whole of the law
Aleister McCrowley, 1999

You. You reading this here editorial. You fucked your mother in an outhouse. You cut the gizzards out of children and fed them to alligators. You smoked crack with Mayor Barry, Farrah Fawcett and Princess Di. And guess what? Nobody gives a fuck.

If you want to have freedom in a media-saturated world you have to learn not to give a fuck about your public image. Be REVOLTING! In fact, have your public image be even more REVOLTING! than *you* are. That way, anything that you might actually *do* will seem mild.

We at REVOLTING! believe in Radical Tabloidism. Random acts of actionable communication straight from the id. Technology has given us this vast shared infospace but there's no freedom of movement because people have been socialized to practice self-censorship. And because our virtual tongues are imprisoned by excessive libel, copyright and trademark restrictions. REVOLTING! intends to bring spontaneity to cyberspace.

CAVEAT
Of course, this whole website is a parody! Don't believe anything we say. Don't get mad. Don't sue us. Don't believe us. Don't be afraid to advertise with us. Don't hate us just because we're REVOLTING! It's all JUST A JOKE heh...

Just Say Nothing
R.U. Sirius Deconstructs the Philosophical Depths of the Now and Near Future Digital Generations

Sometime in 1996, I got into a little tiff in the GenX conference on the Well. Hell if I can remember what it was about, but I noticed the things that I hate about that generation. It motivated several pieces, including the piece on Courtney Love that appeared earlier in this segment. This one is the most explicit piss-take. And why not? It's their turn. The opening quotes actually pretty much cover it.

This brings up a point. Everybody knows that white boomer males are assholes. But did you know that Xers are also assholes? Or that women aren't goddesses while men are schmucks? Women are schmucks too! Non-whites are assholes, probably in ways similar to the way whites are assholes. If you look into this, you'll find it to be true. Just wanted to get that off my chest.

MSNBC's The Site OnLine, April 1997

KNEE-JERK IRONY: The tendency to make flippant ironic comments as a reflexive matter of course in everyday conversation.
DERISION PREEMPTION: A life-style tactic: the refusal to go out on any sort of emotional limb so as to avoid mockery from peers. Derision Preemption *is the main goal of knee-jerk Irony.*

> *-Douglas Coupland,* Generation X

> *The nail that sticks up gets hammered down..*
> *- popular Japanese saying...*

The new age has arrived and—quelle surprise—millions of glowing baby boomers aren't out on the love streets radiating bliss while space brothers hoist Baba Ram Dass up on a caftan weaved of cannabis. Rather, this epoch is characterized by several generations so razor-sharp cynical that they can tell you precisely why something sucks even *before* you tell them what it is. Still, nearly everybody agrees that something has changed. Digital technology has altered everything—where (or whether) we work, how we communicate, what money means, and whether love stinks. Considering this, I decided to examine the philosophical grounding of Generation X and, projecting into the near future, the generations that will follow their rebootheels down the ol' info hypeway.

I've concluded that children of the digital world will live in a philosophic void. This is good. See, there's only so much fun they can have mocking fellow knee-jerk ironists before it all becomes too self-canceling. They'll have to keep baby boomers like me alive, just so they'll have fools to deride.

If, indeed, the philosophy of the digital generations can be reduced to "nothing much," why have I proceeded with this pop deconstructionist quickie? Well, I'm a boomer. These kids will be paying the debts on my orgy of self-indulgence for the rest of their lives. Why not pour salt in the wounds? Right? I mean, should I do this? Yeah, whatever?... Definitely maybe?... heh heh heh.

Ok. Ennui you want it kids, it's all yours. So let's get started.

SELF/IDENTITY

Philosophies of selfhood have (d)evolved over several generations. In this century, we've been through the self-denial of the god-fearing and the Mao-loving. We've been through broadcast media-era, Hollywood/pop star-influenced narcissism. (For amusement, these types can still be observed In Real Space.) Then there's you—the digital generations. Solipsists. Inevitably, the unconscious assumption of the wired up is that a world that's at your fingertips exists entirely for you. Intelligent Agents and bozo filters winnow out materials that might upset this precarious perception of an information universe tailored to your interests. *You* are at the center However, one annoying little glitch reminds you that you're not *really* making the rules. Will you pay that monthly AT&T bill, lest your entire edifice of identity collapses leaving you thoroughly unhinged? You will!

POLITICS

While older Americans define their beliefs in terms of liberal, moderate, and conservative, members of the web generation are defined by those who believe in everything (gray aliens, every conspiracy theory that slithers across the net, ad infinitum) and those who believe in nothing (unless you can tie it in to a snide quip about *The Brady Bunch.*) Someday though, assuredly, a great teacher will arrive. She will astonish the web kids with her new idea: "Some things may be true while others may be false." Whoa! The web kids will ponder this for many nanoseconds. Then they'll flame the living fuck out of her.

CLASS

Class distinctions will grow ever wider. The digital elite, today personified at the extreme by the IPO billion dollar babies, Jerry Yang and Mark Andreeson, will eat up most of the money in the system by manipulating the electronic trading networks like so many tinkertoys. Along with the highly paid digital knowledge workers and webmeisters, this small elite will live like kings among the squalor, although they'll wear snot-covered Depends Undergarments, backwards propeller beanies, and fake leprosy scales—just like everybody else. They'll be called "golden noserings." Everybody else—low-end users with little RAM, no jobs, and no future—will be called... *ORGAN DONORS!*

Observers have noted that with the evolution of a digital/cybernetic culture, the majority of citizens will be economically superfluous. Progress is already being made towards keeping these potentially desperate and angry low-end users off the streets, as local and federal governments enact legislation rendering pretty much everything enjoyable illegal. Soon, the rabble will be safely locked away for life, the seeming injustice of it all rendered painless through the discrete and tasteful use of baseball metaphors.

A few techno-theorists have suggested an alternative plan. The superfluous citizens might be gainfully employed looking at all those web ads nobody else will go near. This option, however, has been criticized as excessively cruel.

PSYCHE

Time, and our attention spans, contracts. Life becomes more disjunctive and discontinuous. Thus, all our moments are experienced without the moderating and relativistic calm of perspective that comes from memory and experience. As Arthur Kroker has noted, our basic psychology is becoming bi-polar, a constant oscillation between ecstasy and dread (wired and *exhausted)*.

With accelerating time— and merciless change and competition—eliminating all psychological comfort zones, Generation X has found a resting place by creating a dead zone. Seizing irony and affectlessness in their once-mighty, RSI-blighted hands, they calm the waters of world historic techno-euphoria and apocalyptic hysteria by insistently trivializing and making silly any and all overexcited transmissions. Triteness is the sedative of the first digital generation. When it fails, there's always heroin.

ARCHITECTURE

Media is getting cheaper and housing more expensive. The large, economically marginalized mass of digital citizens will be essentially homeless and migratory. With Jerry Garcia deceased, they'll need a new subcultural identity to help them feel that their sorry state is a matter of personal choice. The solution?

Building small disposable shelters out of flimsy materials, the organ donor class will use cheap media technologies to create Rave Houses. These "houses" will have the appearance of whatever moving images the occupant chooses to screen, usually cheerful and trippy fractal-mandala meditations.

Naturally, these will become trendy among the golden noserings, who will outdo the organ donors with extraordinary displays of cyberdelic technical virtuosity. While pomo theory types go apeshit with confounding gibberish about the "avant-garde architectural movement," the Government and whatever's left of civil society will be put into crises by the advent of "porn houses" and "ultraviolence houses."

DRUGS/DISCOURSE (WRITTEN IN APPROPRIATELY CONFOUNDING GIBBERISH)

The discourse about drugs has already drugged public discourse, leading inevitably towards the primary philosophic stance of the digital generations—"Just Say Nothing." This started, of course, with Nancy Reagan's "Just Say No." Read literally, this successful slogan doesn't call for behavioral refusal, but instead invokes the wisdom of constraining discourse. Nancy is only telling you what to *say*, and to say *only* that. The more upbeat "Just Do It" equally invokes the wisdom of constraining discourse, this time explicitly in the service of behavioral cooperation. Don't talk about it and don't argue with me. "Just Do It" is militaristic hedonism, a barking command to leap without looking. And a most effective slogan. Joke 1996 Presidential candidate Bob Dole's convoluted attempt at sloganeering, "Just Don't Do It," didn't communicate that one should constrain discourse, but rather that one should constrain behavior. Loser!

It may seem odd that an alleged age of communication is characterized by a constrained discourse. But consider it in the context of temporal acceleration, fragmented attention due to overload (and possibly drugs), and aforementioned GenX strategies for evading commitments to the varieties of hysterical experience. You wind up with that damned surfing metaphor—riding the tip of the wave, skimming the surface of the ocean. Never diving into the depths.

Digital public discourse mimics hard drugs like heroin and cocaine, providing the user with that satisfying druggy experience of an inconclusive, bracketed experience that feels exempt from consequences. The vagaries of wide open net exchanges inevitably, abruptly, decenter any line of inquiry before it gets in too deep. Net conversation compares to a trip on a road where there's too many stop lights with a driver who keeps slamming the brakes and taking sharp turns to get off at every exit—and eventually just veers off in another direction. You quickly learn that you'll never arrive, and readjust your expectations towards a "just say nothing much," destination-free, and probably inconsequential experience.

So, why gather all the information in the universe to leave it to a generation with the attention spans of gnats? That's easy. With the world's information at their fingertips, they won't need to clutter up their pretty little heads with it. Which brings me to...

Sex

Forget about virtual sex. Actual sex allows digital generations to momentarily shift from pure solipsism to solipsism leavened by narcissism. For earlier generations, sex provided an opportunity to moan, grunt, and scare the horses. Thanks to fashion and advertising, sex will be viewed for years to come largely as an opportunity to pout. Earlier generations saw sex as an intense experience, unleashing unconscious emotions. Generations living in cyberspace will look on sex as the only excuse to leave the workstation. In fact, a disembodied culture will see sex as the final repository for experiencing physicality. For most, this will simply involve self-objectification. Using advanced plastic surgery and body modifying drugs, hypersexualized pornographic bodies will be everywhere. From coast to coast, it'll be nothing but *Baywatch*. More extreme types will continue to push the limits of sadomasochism beyond such currently trendy dangerous games as blood sports and autoerotic suffocation. The hipster attitude will be "Live fast, die young, and leave a fuckable corpse."

Life

Life is artificial. Reality is virtual. Sentience is synthetic. The notion that we're working on the machines that will displace us will seize the digital elite by their transcendental short hairs. Uploading before they look, it'll be a simple matter to drag their sorry bitmapped asses into the garbage icon and reboot. After that kids— you're on your own.

Dana Beal and Friends in Search of the Holy Grail

21•C, Fall 1997

ZIPPIES: ONE LETTER UP THE ALPHABET

Flashback 1972: I'm marching with the "Zippies" at the Republican Convention in Miami. Joints are passed as this ragged band of hardcore lunatics strut through a wealthy neighborhood. "FREE CHARLES MANSON!" we chant, while the good men and women of upscale Miami cower in their cars. Some freaks jump on top of the automobiles, middle fingers extended. The teenagers are throwing firecrackers. (They never seem to stop throwing firecrackers. They were throwing firecrackers yesterday, all night long, at the campsite, playing their Alice Cooper and Black Sabbath tapes, drowning out the aging hippies with their folk guitars). And then, here come the riot cops. Lots of them.

It's 1972 now, not Chicago '68, and the Zippies are one letter up the alphabet from the Yippies. Extremism for the hell of it is the theory here, based on Tom Forcade and Dana Beal's interpretation of the science fiction novel *Agents of Chaos* by Norman Spinrad. And Zippies don't stand on ceremony. They immediately assault the officers with flying rocks and bottles. Suddenly everybody is running in all directions, protesters throwing rocks, cops wielding billy clubs. I run like the wind and somehow find myself on an upscale commercial street where I slip inside a bar (filled with law students, it turns out) and order a drink. I spend hours downing scotch and sodas, imagining I'm some kind of Che Guevara, while chatting up the well-dressed liberal law students.

It wasn't right, I suppose, chanting "Free Charles Manson" and throwing rocks—unprovoked—at cops. But it sure was intoxicating. It felt like the French Revolution must have. A fetid mob of rabble gone insane and out for blood.

Fun's fun. But I actually thought the Zippie leaders were kind of dumb. *Agents of Chaos* was rather boring. Dana Beal, the alpha leader of the gang, didn't impress me much. Really, I wanted to be at the Miami Hilton, with the original Yippies, those comfortable sellouts from whom the Zippies had split. Abbie Hoffman, Jerry Rubin, Allen Ginsberg, even John and Yoko(!!) were up there at the Miami Hilton. *There* I would have found an abundance of wit and style, not to mention insight into how to change the world.

Later that night, I'm at the Zippie house somewhere in the Miami ghetto when I hear Dana Beal upstairs throwing a screaming fit. High level Zippie cadre gather and whisper in hushed concern. "This Beal guy sure seems like an idiot." my friend Gary opines, and I agree. Twenty five years later, I find out how wrong I was. Dana Beal is a thinking man's rabble.

A Grab Bag of Wonders

Dana was going over the implications of the rediscovery of Gnostic substances: mind over immune system. *"Miraculous healing, true prophecy, liberation from destructive reflex (sin), victory over death*
The Ibogaine Story: Report of the Staten Island Project
Paul De Rienzo, Dana Beal, & Members of the Project

1997. Dana Beal has been working the streets of America—from the radical left movement that's around ACT UP to the government bureaucrats at the FDA and the NIH—on behalf of a psychedelic drug called Ibogaine. Ibogaine, it seems, is a cure for heroin addiction and cocaine addiction. You take the Ibogaine trip, and when you come down, you don't want junk or toot. No withdrawal sickness. No craving. Nothing.

You see, Howard Lotsof was a junkie himself in the early sixties. A drug pantheist who liked to experiment on occasion with hallucinogens, Lotsof stumbled on some Ibogaine. Told that it was a 36 hour trip, he decided he'd pass, and gave it to a friend. The friend went "completely *sane.*" "That's not a drug. It's a food. We have to tell Congress!" the friend told him. So Howard decided to try it for himself. After 36 hours of harrowing hallucinations that contained "more information about my psychological makeup than twenty years of Freudian analysis," Lotsof discovered an unexpected side effect. His craving for opiates was gone. He couldn't even force himself to work up an enthusiasm for narcotics. Years later, Lotsoff would go on a one-man crusade to get Ibogaine noticed and approved as an anti-addiction medicine.

In fact, Ibogaine might just be a cure for habitual behavior and consumerism. It might just be the direct pipeline to a lucid, straight-talking African wisdom God named BWITI and it might have been Jesus' private email address for talking to the heavenly father.

I digress. But digression is the point. Because Autonomedia has issued an inspiring book, that's as much about the inside of Dana Beal's head as it is about using Ibogaine to cure heroin and cocaine addiction. And we should be thankful for it. *The Ibogaine Story* is a grab bag of wonders that manages to synthesize narcopolitics, Philip K. Dick's *VALIS*, an African deity named BWITI, gnosticism, Black Panther Party politics, cutting edge brain research, quantum mechanics, chaos theory, dream research, and three decades of New York City bohemian street gossip from the Yippies to The Factory to the New York Dolls *to High Times* magazine to CBGB's to the medical marijuana movement.

You see, Ibogaine apparently taps you into this African deity named BWITI. That's the deity's name, and nearly all Ibogaine trippers report imagery that they sense as coming from a distinctly African God, and some even receive the name itself, "BWITI," unprompted. Beal notices that the message of BWITI seems identical to the "Vast Active Living Intelligent System" in P.K. Dick's novel *VALIS*. In *VALIS,* Horselover Flat experiences (among other things) trans-temporality (presence in all times), and has access to precognitive visions. Indeed, those lucky ex-junkies who get to try Ibogaine also frequently evince precise precognition, although you'll never find that in one of

Lotsoff's many reports on Ibogaine testing. It's hard enough to get a visionary plant approved as a cure for bad drugs, no point in bringing precognition into the bargain. Still, one can't help but imagine brokers and speculators lining up to get some, lest their competitors get the competitive edge in the market.

But they would get more than they bargained for, if Beal and other Ibogaine enthusiasts are to be believed. Because Ibogaine seems to not just eliminate the need for dope, it seems to eliminate *the need*. It is conjectured that it eliminates neurosis and consumerism. It's message isn't merely wisdom but right action. As Dick put it in *VALIS*, " 'Do you *know*, now?' 'Yes I know now.' 'So you *know; act* like it!'"

BUT *THIS* MAGICK BULLET REALLY WORKS!

Could Ibogaine be "the breakthrough in the gray room" that Burroughs sought through the disruption of habitual language and thought patterns? Could it dissolve the invisible "Black Iron Prison" that Dick posited in *VALIS*, the one that cut us off from the dreamtime and trapped us in the gray empire of linear time?

With a flourish of old school Zippie-style rhetoric, Beal tells me on the phone that, indeed, he believes that "the changes Ibogaine would unleash would be the system-smash... like a big bang without an explosion."

If this all sounds like the same story that you've heard before about other psychedelic compounds, I suggest that you take a hard look at the evidence, so generously provided. *The Ibogaine Story* is organized as a scrapbook, with Dana Beal in the role of cosmic detective as revolutionary activist, searching for clues that might lead to a real transmutation of the human condition. It's a great big 352 page tome that includes pages of "evidence" torn from *Time* magazine, The *New York Times,* and *Scientific American*. The index includes entire research papers on relevant brain chemistry and on substances closely related to Ibogaine.

A REVOLUTION (IN BRAIN CHEMISTRY)

Meanwhile, over the phone, I try to provoke the bomb thrower in Beal, attempting I suppose to reconnect to my own ultraleftist past as a gun-totin' Zippie supporter of the Weather Underground and the Black Panthers way back in the days when the revolution seemed to be right around the corner. But Beal doesn't bite. His enthusiasm is entirely reserved for plant cures and brain chemistry. A question about political revolt goes ignored. Instead, Dana enthuses about a *New York Times* article that "shows that there's a chemical underpinning to the Christian idea of salvation. And it's based on the fact that the same neurotransmitter, a simplified form of Ibogaine called norharmon—it looks like Ibogaine if you take off a sidechain—*that* is the neurotransmitter of dreams. It does two things. Acutely, it shuts down the entire system during shock and prevents damage. This is how people can be near dead and wake up hours later without damage." We never do get back to the notion of Christian salvation, although the book throws up some Jesus and gnostic Christianity deftly into the mix. He calls me back the next day, and in his usual urgently enthusiastic tone, he imparts this soul saving bit of advice, "MELATONIN! Just take Melatonin every morning at four a.m. It causes some of the same changes to the brain that Ibogaine does." Radical, dude.

The Dope Fiend Manifesto

21•C, Fall 1997
Utne Reader, Winter 1997-1998

I'm really sick of the cliche, propounded by both the natural healing profession and by the medical profession, that we should "listen to our bodies." I propose a more reciprocal relationship. Our bodies should also listen to *us*. In other words, I want my body to cooperate with *my* agenda. I'm not proposing to fight fate with wishful thinking. What I really want is for the medical profession, the pharmaceutical industry, the healing "profession," and the developers of medical technology to move further towards a collaborationist—as opposed to authoritative—relationship with the "patient."

In the 1950s, in the field of psychotherapy, Tim Leary proposed a change in relationship between doctors and patients that has been largely adapted. The therapist would no longer be the one to define optimal psychological health, make judgment on the patient's state, and offer the proscriptive and prescriptive regimens for improvement. Rather, the patient would be presented with a chart defining current behaviors and attitudes. The patient would then define where (s)he wanted to get to, according to a realistic assessment of her potential. The patient would define the goal of the therapy. The therapist would be a "coach," helping the patient get to where she wants to go.

The medical profession needs to make the same transition. I'll make this personal. Right now, I have an ulcer and asthma. These conditions obstruct the life I both want and need. The social lubrication of going out for drinks, for instance, is seriously impeded. I can no longer use stimulants. Leaving pleasure (a perfectly valid need in itself) aside, these denials have consequence. Mixing it up in an alcohol-loosened environment leads to new relationships, connections, opportunities, projects. Occasional stimulants increase *this* writer's productivity, and provides a clarity that results in life-changing decisions.

Recently, I went to several doctors about combating the restrictions on my lifestyle with stronger medicines. Three different Doctors told me that—yes, it would be possible to prescribe stronger medications that might allow me to live more the way I would choose to live without increased suffering. But they weren't going to do that. They were all adamant that the patient must follow the proscriptions for the pathology, and that the *prescriptions* should be secondary. This attitude needs to change.

In my dream life, medical doctors are enthusiastic researchers keeping up with the rapid evolutions and discoveries in medicine, biomedicine, medical technology, natural medicines, ad infinitum. We get together with our Doctors and tell them where we'd like to be optimally, without guilt or taboo. "I'd like to be able to drink one or two glasses of beer with dinner every evening, Doc. I'd like to be able to get an erection five times a day, Doc. I'd like to be able to use a little pick me up a couple of times a week, Doc. And party like a complete maniac on Saturday night." The

Doctor and I put our heads together. He's so well-researched that he knows of a new brain drug—it releases increased vasopressin within any side effects. Another drug, combined with a specific food, counteracts the acidic effects of alcohol consumption. Ad infinitum. Together, we chart a more satisfactory regime.

Crazy Like A Feminist

This sounds like the crazed rantings of a dope fiend, and it is. But so what? The notion that our bodies should conform to *our* agenda is already at the center of feminist and transsexual ideology. Women have insisted on taking control over their reproductive processes. One of the messages of Donna Haraway's notion of "cyborg liberation" is that we use technology to conform to a new set of needs and desires. And in so doing, we change not only power relations but what it is to be human and female. Sex change operations, or breast implants, are further examples of medical procedures that require medical professionals to acknowledge an individual's agenda as taking some precedence over the absolute ideal of risk-free care with intervention only in the case of physical pathologies. In this situation, the Doctor becomes the coach and the patient defines the goal.

Of course, asking society to work towards potentiating autonomous drug taking by reorienting the medical profession away from authoritarianism and towards a collaborationist approach is pretty much tantamount to coupling a taboo and a pariah. But that's ok. This is the age of Jack Kevorkian and Larry Flynt. Just the other side of the neo-morality crusade of the mainstream media, awaits a hailstorm of taboo smashing. Within my lifetime, I expect to be among the first human beings in civilization to be treated as a free adult.

John Perry Barlow Debriefed

Mondo 2000 January 1998

Anarchist, Republican, acid eater, cowboy, Electronic Frontier missionary, sophisticate, *MONDO* contributor, CIA consultant, writer of stentorian Jeffersonian screeds, a man as comfortable rambling the streets with indigent crazies as he is stalking the haunts of the rich and famous.

Barlow showed up on the *MONDO* doorstep as we were just gearing up in '89: a Grateful Dead lyricist, and jack mormon pater familias, fresh from his stint as a married gentleman rancher in Pinedale, Wyoming, and rearing to get into the wind—little did we know how much wind.

That Barlow would accept invitations to lecture the CIA came as no surprise. I mean, we're sophisticated people here. Anyway, we like to think of Barlow as our agent, our man on the inside. Which is why I proposed debriefing him in the pages of *MONDO* and was delighted when he acquiesced.

Beyond an amusing glimpse of the nerve center of the CIA, he doesn't really reveal anything too damaging. I'll accept that it's because he hasn't actually noticed anything too specific. As you'll note, JPB starts waxing philosophical at the drop of a hat. A man like that, always thinking about the big picture, occasionally misses the details. Oh well. *MONDO* has decided that Barlow makes a lousy intelligence agent, but we'll keep him around as a visionary.

GET SMART

R.U. Sirius: You've spoken at a few CIA conventions and advised them?
JOHN PERRY BARLOW: I've been called in on a few occasions to give some back-up to certain forces within the CIA. There's a minority within the CIA who strongly believe they've missed the information revolution in a fundamental way. They realize that they don't understand how information really works. And they're genuine about their mission. Their mission is to try and come up with the most realistic possible picture of what's going on in the world so that the administration can make decisions based on reality rather than fantasy. The problem is that they created a purely Soviet information system. It's completely compartmentalized and has layers and layers of secrecy. And this makes it impossible for them to determine truth, or to have the kind of process where you discover the truth. You want to expose a phenomenon to the widest possible range of peer reviews and different points of view and then come up with a consensus based on what the truth might be. They can't do that because of all the secrecy. So there are some folks now who represent another view. They're very interested in a new open system for both information gathering and dissemination. I was involved in the efforts to get them on the web. You can't imagine how resistant they were to that.

RUS: They *do* have a web site...

JPB: They have a web site and it's chock full of good stuff. If you want to get the latest maps of politically boxy regions like the Balkans, that's the place to go.

Anyway, they're interested in declassifying also. And there's a lot of resistance. The problem is that the whole process of declassification involves shortening the length of so many bureaucratic penises. Inside that system, the way you enlarge your dick is to have the capacity to declare as much stuff secret as possible. The actual sensitivity of the information is far less relevant than your ability to declare it sensitive. And you can imagine what kind of mentality that breeds. One of them said to me, "What we're trying to do is *determine* reality".

So, I got into the nerve center of the CIA. You'd imagine some kind of James Bondian reality... massive parallel computing with the entire world's information and all this secret stuff... But the nerve center of the CIA is five analysts sitting around a great big lazy susan, each of them with a large teletype machine sitting next to them. The teletypes are clattering away, and they tear off these printouts from the teletype machine and put them on the lazy susan, and rotate it around to another analyst who might be interested. It's unbelievably primitive! There are five screens on the wall. When I was there, one of the screens was showing static, and the other four were showing CNN. And while I'm standing there in this supposedly electronically-hardened environment in the nerve center of the CIA, my cell phone rings. (laughter) There was a terrible flurry of embarrassment. I wanted to say, "Yes Ivan, I'm here. Code 9, 11, 10. Blue moon." They're completely inept. They're still passing around information in that building in vacuum tubes, like an old department store.

RUS: They have to be aware that there's been a tremendous technical evolution in information processing. I mean, they're not living in fucking caves!

JPB: There's a little pocket that's quite advanced. But no more advanced than the average Silicon Valley company. If you want to see some genuine technological sophistication, the one thing they do have nailed is satellite systems. They have developed some sophisticated systems. They're taking pictures from space with resolution down to the size of a cigarette pack. The problem is that they have all this information and they don't have any capacity to render it intelligible. They evaluate their effectiveness by how many images they have. So what?! It's like how the Soviets used to evaluate the success of their programmers. They'd weigh the computer chips. (Laughter). They focused so thoroughly on the other side for so long, they became it. There's an old Arab proverb, "Choose your enemies well; for you will eventually become them." That's precisely what happened. The pictures on the wall in the CIA are of scenes inside Russia . Even the wallpaper in some places are old maps of Moscow.

RUS: They're in love.

JPB: They're madly in love, and their lover has died. They're in a profound state of mourning.

RUS: What other insights do you have into the power struggles that are going on there?

JPB: I think the big problem remains the fact that their admissions system is set up to optimize value sets and experience base that are purely those of the WW2 generation. So even though very few members of that generation are still in there, they've only been replaced by people who are able to replicate those value sets. And they're increasingly unusual in society. They're the kids that nobody got along with in school.

RUS: Another group of nerds.

JPB: Yeah. They're socially maladjusted. They're paranoid. They're too smart by half, and they're as straight as you can possibly be in a society that isn't really very straight.

RUS: Militia type publications have been claiming that there's this fifth column in the CIA that's been gathering information on corruption in politics and using it to blackmail corrupt politicians. This is why so many of them have been quitting. Do you know anything about this?

JPB: I'm not privy to this, but I believe it. I think it's one of the reasons that Clinton has been so spineless. It's because they've got him in a lot of ways.

I'll tell you something. When I was around the White House petitioning against the clipper chip (government-sponsored encryption scheme to eliminate freely available public encryption) a few of the people there would confess frankly that they agreed with me. Finally this one guy said to me exasperatedly, "Look. We're more afraid of the NSA than we are of you."

Well, why is the White House afraid of the NSA? Isn't the NSA supposed to work for *them?* Anyway, they're not going to go out and kill him.

RUS: It might have happened once before...

JPB: But it's unlikely. I think it's more that they have files that would be very damaging. This is an old trick...

RUS: The Hoover trick.

CONSPIRACY THEORY

JPB: The Clinton Administration has launched the greatest attack on individual liberties in my lifetime, and that includes the Nixon administration. And it's all been done under the wire and in ways that are so technical and legally obscure that people haven't even noticed. They're doing severe long-term damage to freedom in America in a way that never makes the radar. And people don't know about it. Because it's not the O.J. trial.

RUS.: They have that terrorism bill...

JPB: A beautiful case in point. They pass an anti-terrorism bill after an incident that might have been caused by the Federal government! I'm not paranoid enough to think that they actually blew that plane up in order to keep their jobs. But I'm getting there. You just have to ask yourself— who benefits? Who is going to reap the most from these incidents. It's the obsolete cold war state. That's a lot of people who need to make their car payments. They don't want to quit working. They have to have a justification. And it's not out of the question that some of those people figure they'll produce a justification.

RUS: We're never going to figure out what's going on. It's gotten too complicated. We're never going to know who killed Kennedy, because we're into such a media babel. If you *proved* who killed Kennedy there would still be enough

disinformation around to raise public doubt. **Nobody can get to the bottom line on anything.**

JPB: There are so many wheels within wheels within wheels... Also, the way that information is managed inside that apparatus. It's so compartmentalized. Everybody's sitting on their own little pile of information. There's no way even within the system to gain access to any large percentage of it. I don't care if you're the head of the CIA, there's an awful lot of information that you can't get to.

RUS: I thought about that when John Deutch was denying that the CIA was involved with cocaine. Everybody on the street knows that the CIA has been involved in drug dealing all along... because you know somebody who got mixed up with them somewhere down the line! But maybe Deutch *doesn't* know.

JPB: People on the outside don't get that these organizations *really* aren't great monolithic entities where there's uniformity of knowledge and opinion. They're as filled with internal politics and conspiracies and intrigue as the court of the Medicis. And there's an awful lot going on inside that never sees the surface. You've got to go in to see it. And there are many people inside the CIA that *you* would find compatible.

RUS: I THINK *NOT!* Have you ever talked to your close friend John Kennedy Jr. about the assassination of his father and what his opinion is about who did it?

JPB: Yes. He said he could think about it, but what good would it do it wouldn't change anything. He could go down into that black hole of confusion and anxiety, but he has a life to live. It's unknowable, and if it was knowable, what difference would it make now? He's a healthy guy in a situation that would drive most to psychosis.

No Hippies in the White House

RUS: You've flown on Air Force Two with Gore and talked and hung out with insiders in the Clinton Administration. Tell us about any good or bad weirdness...drug use, closet hardline leftists, sex orgies... anything really weird or interesting.

JPB: Unfortunately, it's duller than you want it to be. I've not been privy to anything really fascinating like internal demons running around loose in the White House. These are all technocrats. Their private lives are just as dull as you'd think. I mean, Al Gore's advance man's a devout Deadhead and Ram Dass' nephew. But he's a very straight young man and a true believer.

RUS: What do they believe *in?* I still can't figure that out.

JPB: I think they believe in benign authority. But once you believe in authority, and once you believe that the Federal government actually connects to the ground in some meaningful way, that justifies a lot of behavior that you wouldn't be able to justify if you looked at things clearly and saw how perversely the effect deviates from the intention. It's not as if the story's connected to the writer.

Newt Mornings

RUS: I have a very unpleasant subject to bring up... Newt Gingrich. You've said some nice things about him. So what is there to like? He wants to hang drug

users in the public square. He's helped to increase the military budget. He tried to censure Torricelli when he brought out revelations about CIA torture in Guatemala. I could go on and on...

JPB: Gingrich is another one of those faces where the balloon he has over his head—the great virtual myth—is greatly at variance with the guy himself. And the characteristics of that balloon have to do not so much with the policies of belief, but the policies of belief that he remains silent about, because he's trying to hold together an incredibly shaky coalition. He's holding together two halves of the Republican party that hate each other. The party consists of fundamentalist authoritarians and *laissez faire* libertarians. And there are some things they agree on about limiting the size of the government and the uselessness of the welfare state as it's been constructed. In a sense, he's trying to do the same thing that Roosevelt did, trying to create a coalition of inner city blacks and Southern racists. They have no natural affinity on many levels, but they have some points of agreement.

RUS: **He's front man for all the individual rights busting draconian crime bills... the prison/industrial complex.**

JPB: I don't want to portray this guy as a hero. I think, in some ways, he's a great person. One of the questions I asked was, "You and I both know that crime has been declining for a long time, but because of television, the perception is that it's increasing. And the people are asking to build more prisons and get tougher on crime. Don't you feel some sense of moral responsibility to do what's right?" And he said, "If I did what was right under these circumstances, I wouldn't be back here."

Dylan Smiles on Misfortune

RUS: **You've spoken in the past about how dark and negative the Grateful Dead were on the inside.**

JPB: Well, really there's a balancing between the Deadheads and the Dead. The lighter and more loving things became out front among the deadheads, the darker and more twisted they became backstage. There was a great sacrifice involved in making that thing go on. After Brett died, the way they dealt with that was so callous and unfeeling. Towards the end, the range of emotional revelation that was allowed inside that family ran the entire gamut from spite to irony. You would never see a man cry. It was simply not done. Or admit to any kind of emotional sensitivity. I was riding from the funeral home to the grave site, and I said, "I'm the only person that can go back and forth between backstage and out front. I'm starting to think that I should pick one or the other. And if I have to do that, I'm going to stay out front. It's a lot safer there." And Garcia said, "Man, if I could do that I would. But, unfortunately, I'm strapped in here."

They're all enormously sensitive as individuals. But they have allowed themselves to become part of a beast that is dark and cold and absolutely heartless. I mourn the Grateful Dead. I lament that I will never have one of those epiphanies that periodically occurred at a Grateful Dead concert. But things had gotten so bad that it was time.

They had gotten used to living in very plush circumstances. They never stayed anyplace but a Four Seasons Hotel. There was a lot of ironically plush living. I can't cast any stones; I was as much a beneficiary as anyone else, and I was delighted by it. It's there, you take it. There was such a strong cultural impetus against judgment and moral imperatives, that it ended up creating a kind of moral vacuum. So there was no awareness of a point where irony crosses over into gross hypocrisy.

RUS: How do *you* locate that line?

JPB: I think there's a lot of truth in that Dylan line "to live outside the law you must be honest." I'm one of the least judgmental people I know. You have to fuck up pretty magnificently before I'll be incapable of finding some extenuating circumstances to get you off the hook. But I do try to have my own personal morality. It's important to me to have a sense of the difference between right and wrong. It's about how you treat people, basically. I don't require that other people share my values, but I do require that I have my own. And they're pretty straight in some ways.

RUS: I heard a hysterical story about the Grateful Dead and Bob Dylan heading to Jerry's funeral. Do you want to tell that story?

JPB: Dylan is the strangest little creature. He's one of those characters that the holy prankster god decides to channel itself through. Further proof that God has a sense of humor. Because it never picks the worthy. It always picks the least likely candidate for the job. And Dylan is inspired, but he's a peculiar little guy. So we're all headed over to Bob Hunter's house after the funeral. I'm driving a rent-a-car, and getting directions from Weir, who was in kind of a strange state. He had been hit unbelievably hard. He knows that something enormous has just happened and he hasn't dealt with it yet. And he's not all that great at directions even in the best of circumstances. And Dylan is in a chauffeured limousine behind us. He's following our lead. And Weir's sending us up all these blind alleys and cul-de-sacs. There's a lot of turning around and going in the other direction and hand waving. Dylan is starting to radiate unhappiness. When Dylan is unhappy, you can feel it two blocks away. And I was thinking, I don't care how weird this guy is he's still the great Bob Dylan and he thinks I'm a complete fuck up. Because he's assuming that since I'm driving, I'm responsible for all this. So I'm pretty embarrassed. Anyway, we finally went up one of those extremely narrow Mill Valley streets and got into a really narrow spot where it was obvious we weren't headed the right way, but the only way we could turn around was to angle ourselves into this driveway. So I'm thinking everything is fine and I drive forward. What I don't know is there's a drop off—some stairs that lead down to somebody's house. And I drive right off this thing. And suddenly the front wheels are pawing air. Everybody in the back seat jumps out and suddenly the car goes boing! and all of it's wheels are off the ground. And it's poised there, teetering back and forth, and threatening to cascade down into these people's front door. We don't know what we're gonna do. We're blocking the street. Cars are coming down. We're all in the street in total distress. Dylan comes out of his limousine, and the look on his face was *so* disgusted.

So I said, "Look, if we all get together here and grab the front end and shove it back while somebody else puts it in reverse, it's possible that we could shove it back along the frame where the front wheels are lifted and pop it back out. So this is what we did and it worked like a charm. I mean, the whole thing didn't take but three minutes. We were in this complete Mongolian clusterfuck one minute and out of it the next.

Of course, Dylan wasn't about to be part of the team that popped the car out—there were six or seven guys, some of them passersby trying to get past us down the street, so it was an odd collection of folk. But the moment we were reaching out to make this great effort and push the car back out of danger, I turned around and there was Dylan about five feet behind us with the strangest smirk on his face. It was the only time I've seen the little asshole smile. So as soon as we got the car up and out, I looked to see what his reaction was. And he immediately spun on his heels and was headed back toward his limousine without giving us the grace of any appreciation.

TechnoSurrealism

DisInformation (www.disinfo.com) March 1998

EVERYONE IS A COMPLETE *DISAPPOINTMENT!'*
    John Giorno

You're idea is crazy, but it isn't crazy enough to be true.
    Neils Bohr

Technoculture, or cyberculture as it is called in the vulgate, has been through four ideational stages. The purpose and intention of this document is to announce the fifth. These ideational stages are:

1) Pure Nerdism 1976-1988
2) Technoanarchy (the MONDO 2000 epoch) 1989-1992
3) Technolibertarianism (the Wired epoch) 1993- March 12, 1998
4) Technorealism March 12 - March 19, 1998
5) TechnoSurrealism March 20, 1998 - Dec 21, 2012

1) Pure Nerdism (1976-1988)
Technoculture was truly a small subculture in these early days. Nerds had some shared beliefs and ethics, like the much maligned "Information wants to be free." Ironically, they didn't particularly care about *sharing* them. They were not interested in getting terribly involved with politics (or girls). They were too busy hacking to pontificate. They weren't into hype.

Then I came along

2) Technoanarchy: the MONDO 2000 epoch (1989-1992)
In this glorious epoch, my friends and I induced confused, stoned youths in the thousands (well, maybe hundreds) to wander soul-naked and bloody starkers raving mad into the badlands of cyberspace. It was a time of great exuberance and imagination as we apprehended and celebrated the media anarchy implicit in the vastness and chaos of the digital terrain. And it was a time of great gibberish when fractal geometry and chaos theory could be wielded to induce people to write for five cents per word. Nobody questioned the wisdom of the technoanarchist avant-garde.

After all, we were all on smart pills.

3) Technolibertarianism: the *Wired* epoch (1993 - March 12, 1998)
And then, suddenly, any Republican post-industrialist corporate boomer in possession of more imagination than the average accountant was presented before the

just-now-forming digital masses as a wild anti-government visionary. What cable TV subscriber could resist the curious pull of such counterintuitive statements as "VIACOM DOESN'T SUCK"? Who could fail to be fascinated by a libertarian magazine campaigning against state control and excesses in copyright, while employing an expensive, pitbull legal team to enact a campaign in defense of its trademark that threatened to colonize the entire English language? And who could resist cyberNewt Gingrich and the Republican Revolution as they mustered whatever political power they could; from corporate America's over-taxed tills, from her heroic anti-drug warriors, from her poor huddled underfunded defense establishment, in order to fight the good fight against the black teenage mothers who so ruthlessly dominated this great (if soon to be obsolete) nation state?

4) Technorealism (March 12-19, 1998)
It had become apparent that, after two consecutive epochs wired on hyperbolic technobabble, the intelligencia needed to crash. So a small group of intellectuals bent on truth and a book contract had a brilliant... er... um... at least sobering idea: What if we were to continue the trend, and make each digital epoch more dreary than the last? What if we were to lay claim to digital reality itself, defining it in language so stilted, with ideas so mind-numbingly simplistic and obvious, so soporific that a dazed cyberpopulis, already rendered doofus from data shock, might just sign on? And in the course of cyberevents, both great and small, we may sufficiently impress Random House or perhaps St. Martin's Press?

The TechnoSurrealist Manifesto
And ever since I have had a great desire to show forbearance to scientific musing, however unbecoming, in the final analysis, from every point of view. Radio? Fine. Syphilis? If you like. Photography? I don't see any reason why not. The cinema? Three cheers for darkened years. War? Gave us a good laugh. The telephone? Hello. Youth? Charming white hair. Try to make me say thank you: Thank you. Thank you.
Andre Breton, The Surrealist Manifesto

Consensus reality is dead! Watch your overcoat.

Forget Technorealism
Forget Technorealism. Realism without imagination is mere reductionism. Realism is not a realistic response to accelerating change. As we approach the apotheosis of the interpenetration of human lives and media, and anarchic democratic access to the means of communication, we sense the eruption of levels of mediated cognitive chaos that is beyond our abilities to comprehend, predict, or define. And while tenured academics might dream of slowing this digital demon down that it might be parsed in a spirit of Amish-like rectitude, there is no solid ground upon which to examine the corpus of current techno-sociopolitical reality. The whole notion of a shared consensus, some kind of social center, is decaying at a fever clip and youths raised on the net and the web won't even recognize the cultural and political assumptions that are still parroted today, albeit with less and less conviction

Attempts to reverse undesirable trends of *real* importance, like the increasing gulf between the rich and the poor, or the fact that a nation of pod people will tolerate corporate testing of bodily fluids without screaming bloody revolution, are not serviced by a tepid set of rationalist principles aimed at unseating a small, perceived techno-utopian elite whose influence is limited and waning anyway. Pay attention to the rabble, on the streets or on the web. Then you'll understand that the primary political polarity of our age isn't technolibertarians vs. neo-Luddites, it's between those who believe in everything (gray aliens, The Gnomes of Zurich and every conspiracy theory that slithers across the net, ad infinitum) and those who believe in nothing (unless you can tie it in to a snide quip about *The Brady Bunch* or *Mork and Mindy*). And both sides are, implicitly, supporters of TECHNOSURREALISM. Whether they know it or not.

THE PROBLEM OF MONEY

Digital communication is a dissipative, boundary-disrupting tool. I won't bore you repeating the old arguments about how the net - and mediated communications culture itself - puts intellectual property, the nation state, the money system, even the well-defined self, into crisis. You can read the back issues of *Mondo 2000* and *Wired* yourselves. It should be enough to simply remind people that just because a situational description has grown tiresome through repetition, or has been adapted by people whose political leanings you don't particularly like, that doesn't make it untrue. And I apologize to all of the writers who, like myself, are struggling within the economics of digital capitalism, but you are going to have to struggle for an end to society being organized around economics, *not* for greater copyright protection! (When photographers for 24 Hours in Cyberspace took pictures of the Zapatistas, Subcomandante Insurgente Marcos thought the pictures should belong to the *photographer's subject.*). You can't count beans in a flood, and you shouldn't *want* to, all right?

Throughout the 20th century, starting with the Dada/Surrealists, individuals who were too alive and imaginative to stomach *horseshit* have argued for an end to wage slavery, This was premature in the 1930's. In the digital age, it's absolutely *necessary*. The solid, secure, agricultural/industrial era, production-oriented forms of labor have been displaced by automation and dissipated by the global work force. There has never before been a time in history where a majority of people have been forced to hustle so pointlessly, toiling the fields of hype, poisoning the real and conceptual environment with utterly bogus product, desperately servicing invented needs, building massive unnecessary arsenals, clearcutting the forests, and always demanding that their self-interests, however obsolete, be protected, *instead* of demanding the transformation of a social system that will make them do *anything* for money, even ask Big Brother to reach into the privacy of individual homes to make sure nobody is copying anything for free, which is the *only* way to carry traditions of intellectual property into the high tech world. I'll say it once more, straight out: The whole situation around information as property *isn't* resolvable. We need a social system that doesn't require artists and software writers (or anybody) to make money.

Is anybody with me? Of course you are.

INFORMATION WANTS TO BE FREE AND SO DO I
You must have chaos in your soul to give birth to a dancing star.
Nietzsche

This is the decade of the tight asshole. Intellectuals who you presumed to be at least 50% sane will suddenly start justifying the de facto censorship of a film based on a book by Nabokov. Seems that every time you turn around, someone else is buying or selling a huge bale of horseshit in the name of social responsibility. A stifling, smug centrism trickles down like day-old piss, from that horndog in the White House to the blockhead in each of us. The next person who bores me gets a Ketamine dart between the eyes. I've done all I can with language. The age of technosurrealism has already exceeded the Age of Reason and now it is over, too. Go home to your husbands, wives and children. Reality is a stranger to us all.

| Introduction | Documents | Volunteer! | Multimedia | **The Revolution** |
| Platform | Events | Networking | Updates | Think really differer |

START THE REVOLUTION (WITH OR) WITHOUT ME
R.U. Sirius Announces a Post-Modern Social Contract and a Political Party for the Rest of Us

Disinformation www.disinfo.com

Beautiful is the chance encounter, on an operating table, of a sewing machine and an umbrella.
Lautreamont

It stands to reason that self-righteous, inflexible, singleminded, authoritarian true believers are politically organized. Open-minded, flexible, complex, ambiguous, anti-authoritarian people would just as soon be left to mind their own fucking business.
R.U. Sirius, from How To Mutate & Take Over The World

We're stuck, you and I. We would just as soon be out on the beach with a fine wine, some Nietzsche, and a drum'n'bass deconstruction of *Exiles On Main Street* tuning in to eternal questions regarding life, mortality, sexuality and so forth. But we live in a world of politics (sometimes called economics) from which there is no escape, no permanent autonomous zone. And so we must use politics to end politics. Thus, I am starting a political party for those of us who would really rather not. How gauche, you say. And I agree. Politics is terribly unfashionable and tacky. It is with great embarrassment that I embark on this endeavor. But consider this: public embarrassment is to cyberspace what skydiving is to the jaded middle class... or something. Let us begin.

PART ONE:

THE POST-MODERN SOCIAL CONTRACT
Whereas <u>Your Name Here</u>, although a conceptually-rugged individualist, seeks some small degree of protection from a rampaging police state, excessive multinational corporate domination, poverty, endless litigation and legalities, and *even* ideologically pure libertarians and anarchists, and testifying that I—of my own free will and not currently under the influence of bad drugs from untrustworthy sources—have chosen to make known my philosophic agreement with "The Post-Modern Social Contract" as laid forth in the rest of this document.

This 21st Century social contract shuns ideologies, *even* nihilism, and instead operates under a basic premise that there are a few simple, loosely-help principles that *maybe* humans would do well to follow if they wish—as we the undersigned *sometimes* do—to survive and thrive on this planet, pending other travel arrangements.

® Think *really* different!

This contract further commits <u>Your Name Here</u> to some nominal effort, perhaps but not necessarily expended on Sunday evenings after *The Simpsons, King of the Hill,* and *X Files* on Fox, on behalf of the fulfillment of this Post-Modern Contract, which we the undersigned will achieve through some sort of heuristic process that engages all possible forms of intelligence, analyses, hysteria, artistry, salesmanship, tenacity, whoring, campaigning, drinking, shiatsu massage, cross-dressing, musicianship, occult rituals, conspiring, gourmet cooking, slimy media productions appealing to the lowest common denominator, or any form chosen by <u>Your Name Here</u> as a contribution to The Revolution®, the "Political Party" that shall represent the Post-Modern Social Contract in the sadly-banal-yet-somehow-challenging world of Machiavellian realpolitik in the 21st Century. (The 20th Century is conceived here as having already ended with the death of Sinatra.)

The Post-Modern Social Contract agrees, in essence, that 21st Century Government (which must exist until such times as all humans are wealthy and secure enough to be completely self-governing), as a representative of both the democratic will of the people and a guarantor of maximum liberty for the individual, should seek to do *good* things that help make it possible for individuals to live as well as they might before they go altogether whilst not doing *bad* things that strip individuals of personal freedoms or that unfairly advantage the a-human structures known primarily as multinational corporations, which currently own the so-called democratic process. We the undersigned acknowledge that this is a crazy, bizarre and obscure notion and that the mainline political discourse, as well as most alternative political discourse presumes instead a debate between those who say that there is Too Much Government (argument taken to new heights of hypocrisy by the "Republican Revolution) and those who, like Democratic Senators Waxman and Lieberman, seek to legislate everything right down to making sure I don't stand up in my tub, fall over, and hurt my head.

In its place, the Post-Modern Social Contract suggests a heuristic movement towards achieving many of the goals associated with Liberalism and Libertarianism while evading and avoiding the politically correct absolutes associated with these tendencies.

It is therefore agreed by <u>Your Name Here</u> , signee of The Post-Modern Social Contract, that an advanced high technological social system will lift all persons above impoverishment *unconditionally* while at the same time seeking to guarantee the least possible intervention of Government in the lives of individuals, *even* their economic lives.

<u>Your Name Here</u> further agrees that those who say that better social well-being and more individual freedom are incompatible shall from this point on be referred to as "Yee Of Little Imagination," and I shall challenge Yee of Little Imagination to look past his or her nose, except when I really don't feel like it or I'm otherwise preoccupied trying to score for sex, or if Yee is armed or awfully huge and aggressive.

72

Finally, <u>Your Name Here</u> agrees to examine R.U. Sirius' initial proposed 15 Point Plan offering a new national political agenda for the USA and after overcoming my shock that this is awfully serious and almost pragmatic, and with the additional understanding that all points are vastly oversimplified and R.U. has probably already thought through all of my objections because like the glorious chairman who swam the Yangtzee River, his shit glows in the dark and is blessed by the mysterious war god Nyaaabrag and his wife Lalala Nicelady, that if I can agree *essentially* with at least 10 of the 15 points, I will JOIN THE Revolution®! On joining, I will contribute towards its ultimate success via such thoroughly legal means as private and public argumentation, media propagandizing, and electoral politics. I further agree that I shall deny before the FBI or any Senate Subcommittee any knowledge of secret guerrilla training camps in the Swiss Alps, financed by Mohammar Khadafy, and under the leadership of R.U.'s brother, the Great and Terrible Hassan I Sirius, who utilizes a technique involving tantric masturbation to hardcore pornography while high on DMT to brainwash a group of ecstatic warrior-assassins who are ready and waiting to seize power By Any Means Necessary should The Revolution® by legitimate means fail, for this is all rumor and innuendo and completely untrue.

Therefore I, <u>Your Name Here</u>, do solemnly swear that Sirius would have charmed the pants off me with this crazy blather were I wearing any, and thus, naked as a jaybird and only mildly intoxicated on Plum Wine or perhaps not at all, I agree to this Post-Modern Social Contract or alternatively perhaps; I, <u>Your Name Here</u>, actually find Mr. Sirius quite irritating, but having skipped ahead and having read his 15 Point Program for The Revolution® I find myself agreeing with most of it, so I'll sign this Post-Modern Social Contract and plot to convince the far more amusing; A) Michael Moore B) Subcommandante Marcos C) Sandra Bernhardt D) Paul Krassner to take up the cause as leader of The Revolution® in a grass roots upheaval that leaves Mr. Sirius a broken man.

In any case, consider me a signee of the Post-Modern Social Contract and a member of The Revolution®. I agree to contemplate tithing 5% of my income to The Revolution® if and when they set up tax deductibility, although I'm quite sure that I'll reject that notion.

THE Revolution® Part II: A Political Party

Religion is poison, sure. Hey man. So is ideology.
Yippie MauMau of Tibet, 1969

We need history because it is the storage closet in which the costumes are kept. We are the first era that is truly learned so far as "costumes" are concerned—we are better prepared than any time has ever been for the Great Carnival, the most spirited Mardi-Gras laughter, the most reckless fun, for the transcendental summit of the utmost idiocy, for a truly Aristophanean mockery of the universe. We can be the parodists of world history, the punchinellos of God! If nothing else living today has a future—perhaps it will be our laugher that has one.
Nietzche

We're unmaking history here!
Hassan I Sirius, email to Lisa-Marie Presley

PRE-RAMBLE:
In 1996 I ran for President.

Ok. I *walked*, actually.

Honestly? I laid down. I was high on morphine one evening at a Chinese Restaurant in Berkeley while the UnDemocratic Convention was busy coronating President Groovy and his stiffy (Al Gore.) It appeared in front of my imagination in flashing neon like a Jenny Holzer electronic sculpture: DERISION 96: FUCK THE VOTE!

I couldn't shake it. It was a perfect slogan. And that ought to have been enough. I mean, consider the alternatives.

I imagined the disenfranchised masses rising up. Concerned pundits driven to apoplexy because everywhere Clinton, Dole, and Perot went there would be a crowd of lunatics shouting "R.U. Sirius?!!" What other possible response to the politics of the moment? There would have been copulating in the voting booths. Dan Rather's electronic circuits would have sizzled and smoked in astonishment as I blipped onto the radar screen. 1%... one lousy fucking percent was all I asked!!!

Fuck 'Em If They Can't Take A Joke or
When the Going Gets Wired the Weird Turn Sirius

It didn't catch on.

I want to propose to you. That's right, *you* with the microchip up your sphincter. And the rest of you too... even the one's who write me email saying stuff like, "I agree with what you're saying about total Revolution and free food, needles, and condoms, but why didn't you say anything about the face on mars?"

74

Let's play a game. Let's play wonk. Let's imagine that we actually have the power to make policy in this Democracy.

I'm going to run a serious campaign this time.

For the moment, let's call it the "Alternative Party." *(Note to Richard: I'm changing the name to The Revolution®, because I really like the chicken burritos [without the onions] at Taco Bell. And I figure that if they're advertising revolution right now, it's gotta be mass market.)* I know... lame. But hang with me for a moment. I wanna get some votes in this election, not just please a handful of too-hip-to-breathe compatri-ots with pictures of Lynette "Squeeky" Fromme and Antonin Artaud on their computer monitors. I want *millions* of votes. And I figure; if we can have an alternative music, if we can have an alternative culture that's embraced by Volkswagen and Jordache Jeans, why can't we have an Alternative Party and get at least half as many votes as Eddie Vedder sells CDs? Are you following me? Am I making sense here? *(Note to Richard: I think this still makes sense. We can hype The Revolution® in the context of 90s content-free bohemianism. "Get a cappuccino at Starbucks and then Vote The Revolution®!" Voting radical as a fashion accessory. How can it miss?)*

Perry Farrell can organize the campaign tour. Reebok and Nike will battle Coke and Pepsi for the opportunity to endorse. In fact, this may be an ideal way to avoid the trap of being beholden to dozens of wealthy and powerful financial contributors. We will *instead* be beholden to just one sponsor. Let's say it's Reebok. I agree that, for instance, if I'm elected President I will wear Reeboks everywhere. I wear the logo on my t-shirt during State dinners, press conferences, etc. We paint the Reebok logo on the front of the White House. During the inauguration ceremonies, Monica Lewinsky will appear wearing naught but a lovely pair of Reeboks. Replace the stars on the flag with the Reebok logo. We give Reebok all of the advantages that other politicians give all their contributors. But then we're free to *screw* all the other mega-corpora-tions if and when we see fit.

Looking further down the road, I can imagine sponsorship replacing taxation. Three decades ago, corporations carried more than 30% of the tax burden. Now corpora-tions carry less than 10%, and we all have to make up the slack. But what if we could trick the corporations into sponsoring social programs and infrastructure. "Alabama's Generous Food Stamp Program is Brought to You By Burger King." Ok, I know... further down the road, as I said.

The Revolution® 15 POINT PARTY PLATFORM FOR NATIONAL POLITICS

NOTE: All of these platform points are stated simply in three-or-less sentences. The reality would be far more complex. I'm not going to nerd out here with details and qualifiers. What I *will* be doing is detailing in each one of these, one by one, in the months to come

1) We will repeal five times as many laws as we pass. We need to simplify and clarify the rules of the game. We will do a better job of enforcing and obeying a few reasonable rules than thousands upon thousands of incomprehensible statutes.

2) End *all* corporate welfare. Let allegedly-free enterprise stand on its own two feet.

3) No Federal Personal Income Taxes for individuals with incomes of less that $100,000. Encourage states and counties to also end taxation of middle-class and poor individuals. Institute a flat tax on income over $100,000.

4) Legalize most pleasure drugs, prostitution, and gambling. Institute a "sin tax," taxing these activities at 100% to make up for some of the funds lost as the result of #1. Use part of this tax income to make counseling and rehabilitation easily available in all locales.

5) Close down the prison/industrial complex. Pardon all prisoners who are in for non-violent crimes involving sums involving $25,000 or less, provided they have no known history of violent activities. Pardon all prisoners listed with Amnesty International.

6) Defend civil liberties. For the first time in recent memory, let's have a federal government that respects The Constitution and The Bill of Rights. Let's have the ACLU and the EFF and other pro-rights organizations inside the federal government.

7) Stop policing the world. Become just another member of the UN, with responsibilities equivalent to our numbers. Reduce the Pentagon Budget by at least 50%.

8) Close down the National Security State. Since the end of World War 2, representative democracy has been hostage to the National Security State. Release all secret documents (excluding only those recent ones that present a very clear and present danger), fire the CIA, and reform the federal intelligence apparatus.

9) Put environmental concerns before profits *and* jobs. On the other hand, put scientific consensus and reason ahead of emotional-based environmentalism. Protect the environment while limiting Orwellian bureaucratic absurdities.

10) Open federally-funded birth control clinics all across the country, guaranteeing women in every locale reasonable access to her legal right to access to abortion and other forms of birth control.

11) Allow "autonomous zones." Offer ways in which localities and even households can —with a very few limits — opt out of the system.

12) Re-establish social services at pre-Reagan levels, for starters. Study the possibility of a "workfare" state that would create an ultimately self-sustaining "generic"

maintenance economy that would involve those who don't receive income independently, or through employment, in the production, distribution, and receivership of life's essentials. Ultimately, an advanced high tech society will need to end the employment/make money ethic entirely or risk a total psychotic break from the social/environmental pollution wreaked by billions of desperate people on a hustle.

13) Study the possibility of restructuring the economic/money system toward making money consistent with actual value in an age where money-as-information is excessively abstracted from the creation of real wealth and unfairly favors those who know how to manipulate it. Also, question the oligarchic power of those who control the money system, such as the Federal Reserve, the IMF, and the World Bank, reforming or possibly eliminating those organizations.

14) Fund a "Manhattan Project Toward Utopia." Finance and encourage altruistic scientific and technological projects geared towards breakthroughs that can diminish or eliminate scarcity, disease, and other forms of suffering that most people would prefer not to experience. Establish a principal of universal access to the products of such breakthroughs.

15) Victory Over Horseshit!*** The political process in America is hostage to certain obvious absurdities that are an embarrassment before the civilized world; like the continuing embargo against Cuba (and particularly the Helms/Burton bill), the excessive numbers of state executions, our refusal to sign the land mine treaty, the opposition to policies like needle exchange that are geared towards slowing down a plague, refusal of funding for international birth control, ad infinitum. Let's have a national government that calls ridiculous horseshit what it is.

What Is To Be Done
It's all a monstrous joke! It's serious. I'm Sirius. Can we MAKE FUN and still get serious political change on the public agenda? Can we do it any other way than by making fun?

I hope that volunteers will come forward to help put this party together. Let me be honest. I haven't done a fucking thing, other than write this thing that's in front of you. Like most of you, I've been busy trying to keep alive.

Needs include; researchers to do the detail work on the platform. Researchers, or people with a working knowledge of the political system, to delineate and deal with the legalities of forming a political party, getting on ballots, fundraising, etc. Fundraisers. Members. Media coverage. Lecture invitations. Endorsements from the famous and the fashionable. Advocates. Avocados. Cans of tuna fish. Pencils. Ad infinitum.

Wouldn't it be fun if a group of non-ideological, non-purist, fun-loving non-believers actually mounted a campaign to end oppression, just to see if it might work? Could be the best role-playing game you've ever tried.

****

Final Notes

* If you want to become a volunteer, as well as a member, and get involved with research, fundraising (eventually), organizing lectures and live appearances, generating media, organizing signature drives, and confounding mainstream politicians, write VOLUNTEER next to the Subject header when you send me email to rusirius@well.com

** If you just want to become a member, writhe MEMBER next to the subject header

*** VICTORY OVER HORSESHIT was originally the slogan of Art Kleps' Neo-American Church, a religious organization started by a psychedelic prankster extraordinaire in the 1960s.

JOIN THE REVOLUTION®! at www.the-revolution.org!!!!!!!!

Technology is a Trickster God: an Interview
with Erik Davis

Salon   October, 1998

I first noticed Erik Davis in the early nineties when I read a piece he'd written about UFO literature for *the Village Voice*. Besides being the first uncynical yet smart piece about this phenonenon I'd encountered since I'd stumbled across Jung's writings on the subject many years before, his poetic use of language in the expository form was nothing short of exquisite. Since then, Davis has kept his sharp-yet-expansive intelligence focused on the various flavors of millennial strangeness that permeate our digitized era.

His current book, *TechGnosis,* casts a wide net, elucidating both the historical context and the meaning behind digital gnosticism, technopaganism, Gibson's voudoun-haunted visions of cyberspace, the extropian dreams of disembodied immortality, cyberdelia, and most of the other odd phantoms of mind and spirit that seem to turn on the strange tribes on the edges of technoculture. This territory has been explored before by the likes of Doug Rushkoff and Mark Dery, but it has never been so eloquently explained. Over the week of October 12, I pestered the busy Mr. Davis for further explications. The results appear below.

R.U. SIRIUS: On the fringes of technoculture, there's always been a link made between digital technology and spirituality, or mysticism. Most commentators have written it off as mere eccentricity, but your book manages to make it all sound rather reasonable. Still, if you had to explain what that link is in a sound byte, or at least in a couple of minutes, what would you say?
ERIK DAVIS: *TechGnosis* sets out to prove that technology and spirituality don't exist in totally separate regions of human culture. That's just not true. Modern technology is built on premodern dreams, whether Christian hopes for the New Jerusalem or animist ideas about electricity and the life force. Those dreams now lurk in the margins, in what I call the technological unconscious, but they continue to inform the fantasies, expectations, and ideas that surround technology. For example, modern advertising is essentially a magical system of inducements deployed through technology. And it's not simply an accident that occult material, however hackneyed, figures so predominantly in computer games.
RU: Ok. You're talking here primarily about technology emerging from spirituality. What about the reverse of that? Over the last century or so, human beings have taken flight, projected their voices and images across space and time, and done a whole host of other things that earlier humans would have found (in the words of Arthur Clarke) indistinguishable from magic. And these things have stirred the transcendental hopes and imaginings of moderns as well. But are they actually magic?

ED: Well, that's a tricky question. It depends what you mean by magic. Ioan Couliano, the religious scholar who was Eliade's greatest student, made the point that modern technology realizes dreams first imagined by earlier generations of magicians. That's one way of interpreting Clarke's famous quip. The fact that these things came about through the rational exploitation of natural law may be less important than we tend to think, because the social and cultural effects of technologies are often quite irrational, even mythical. One of the main aims of the book is to illustrate this. On the other hand, even if 20th century technology mobilizes these transcendental imaginings, subconsciously or not, they are also simultaneously "profane" and utterly removed from the sacred in any traditional sense. That's the Promethean irony, the dark parody, of techno-mysticism. Jacques Ellul made this point as well: the machine generates ecstasy, but mechanizes it as well.

RU: On the other hand, if combinations of digital technology, biotech, nanotech, and other technoscientific forces are modifying who, or *what* we are, what is sacred or profane might be up for grabs. Also, from the point of view of the jester or prankster, the profane is frequently sacred because it punctures the pomposity that gets attached to sacredness. Comments?

ED: Well you're of course plugged into the playful animating spirit of *TechGnosis*. The archetypes that dominate technological culture today are either angelic or demonic — the New Jerusalem of the techno-utopians or the evil Faustian Frankenstein monsters of the Neo-Luddites. But in my view, technology is more like a trickster: it scrambles established codes, overturns truths, and constantly hoodwinks us with unintended consequences. And that's especially true of communication technology. Remember, Hermes, the Greek god of messages, is both a trickster and a magician.

All the technological developments you name are pointing towards a future where mind — whatever that is, and we shouldn't think for a moment that the cognitive scientists have any more of a clue than you do — can manifest itself in matter with greater and greater ease. Obviously this means values are up for grabs. But I suspect that some basic human questions, common to both practical spirituality and modern humanism, will still play a vital role in guiding our increasingly technological society. The trickster is not the only god around.

RU: Could you expand on that? What questions, what practices, and what gods are most likely to emerge in a technoculture?

ED: Ok. We know that information technology is changing consciousness. But the way it's coupled with the current climate of late capitalism, it's happening in a mostly banal way. We find ourselves living with a more multi-tasking, scattered, data-rich, and high velocity mind. We need to work with that mind, but also to recognize its profound limitations. Attention is the key, and any practices that refine attention will become valued in a technoculture like ours.

Now, to put on my pointed prophet's hat for a brief moment, I'd say that fringe groups like Heaven's Gate and Aum Shinrikyo will continue to mix up apocalyptic expectations and technology. The possibilities of artificial life and machine consciousness will also stir up all sorts of fears, fantasies, and polytheistic projections, as we become more and more seduced into anthropomorphizing our increasingly animated machines. But the real questions will be raised by biotechnology and genetic engineering. We really *are* becoming posthuman, and I can't see how we can face the extraordinary turbulence and terror of this moment without asking fundamental questions about what the hell we are here for in the first place. Hard-headed humanists want those questions answered in utterly utilitarian and scientific terms; my book suggests that this rationalist fantasy may be the biggest myth of all.

RU: Do you have a personal technospiritual practice?

ED: Well, as I explain in my book, I think one modern idea of spiritual practice — techniques as opposed to beliefs or religious dogma — emerges partly from our experience as people deeply influenced by the pragmatic and do-it-yourself spirit of technology. We are bricoleurs of the spirit. Even the Buddha talked about his path as a kind of raft provisionally lashed together from flotsam and weeds, only to be abandoned on the other side. I just think we never get to the other side, and that our raft is constantly leaking. And so I'm interested in studying anything that helps me understand how "I" come to be: neuroscience, evolutionary psychology, cultural history, even advertising.

I think we're only just beginning to explore the kinds of technologies, like groupware, VR, and advanced biofeedback, that will really build interesting "platforms" for consciousness. Personally I'm no longer quite as interested in brain machines... or even neurotropics.

RU: Say it ain't so! (laughter)

ED: Well, who knows what tomorrow will bring. I certainly haven't hung up the sword of psychedelia. But right now I'm really into more basic techniques that awaken and alter our immediate experience: meditation, breathwork, and mindfulness of the feedback loops between body and mind. That kind of moment-to-moment attention to perception and experience applies to every aspect of life, including our deeply strange relationships with technology and media. I see the web as a Rorschach blot; automobiles as surrogate selves. E-mail lists are amazing places to watch yourself: why do you post? who do you think you're responding to? why is bug-eyed anger so close to the surface of digital disputes? Everything is grist for the mill. Even *South Park*. Ummm... scratch that. *Especially South Park.*

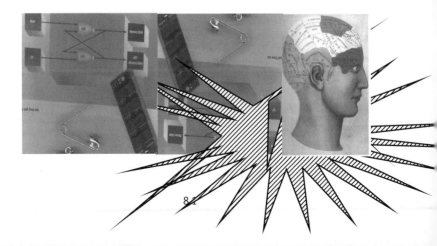

CHAPTER TWO:

TRIPPING OVER THE (NEW) EDGE

Introduction to Chapter 2

I wasn't *really* naive when I started the puckish, upbeat, psychedelic high tech magazine called *High Frontiers* in 1984. I'd already been an early seventies "street fighting man" with friends in the Weather Underground, a mid-seventies proto-slacker street nihilist, a punk/funk vocalist, and an occasional misogynist with a taste for femme fatales. But on some deep level, I felt propelled forward by a positive vision of a neopsychedelic renaissance that would be spurred on by the new technology. A rave was still something like a rant and the bourgeois-anarchist technotopianism of *Wired* was a full decade away. And there I was with high hopes that somehow a discourse that enclosed Blakean visions with the raw beginnings of digital technology, that married the ponderings of quantum physicists with the desires of post-scarcity anarchists, that combined irrepressed expressions of yipping joy with an ascerbic anti-authoritarian undertow—would somehow transmute our social reality into something I could tolerate living in.

I still "preach" from the same book to a degree. I still advocate an end to the economics of scarcity (using a combination of technology and politics to get there) and I honor the visions and insights made possible by the positive, intelligent use of psychedelic plants and chemicals. But I'm skeptical about the world-changing possibilities of a psychedelic renaissance. And I've become extremely cynical about the human animal in general. My position now is that we probably have the technology and resources now to end scarcity and make life a lot more pleasant. In fact, within two or three decades it probably won't even require much political will to make this a reality. But even if we do, lots of people will still be assholes.

At the end of the 1980s, *High Frontiers* mutated into *MONDO 2000*. Right from the start, *MONDO 2000* provoked a more powerful response than anything that I've been involved with, before or since. We'd worked six months on designing the first "cyberpunk" issue. I mean, we worked every day, half-a-dozen of us. It was like making a movie. It had to be just right. (Looking back, there's a lot that's naive in the first edition of *MONDO*. But it still stands as a compelling document linking the cyberpunk SF sensibility to psychedelic utopianism and the Silicon Valley hacking elite.) We didn't have the money to go to press, so we made Xerox copies of the edition and we brought it to a "Hypermedia" Conference at Moscone Center in San Francisco. We had sixty copies that we were selling for an unusually high price (I don't remember, exactly) and they went within a few hours of the first day! We knew we were on to something. We also sent a copy to Stewart Brand, hoping he might help us locate a funding source. He liked it enough to finance the Xeroxing of 80 copies to send to his exclusive Global Business Network mailing list. That was the first I ever heard of the infamous GBN, the avant-garde think tank that sells abstract ideas to corporate leaders and is now associated in most people's minds with *Wired*.

When Queen Mu got a family inheritance (much less than most people imagine), it was off to the races. The magazine grew fast, doubling circulation over the first three issues and selling out its print runs. We were the hit of independent zines. Not *really* mainstream (our circulation eventually topped out just shy of 100,000) but mainstream enough to make us appear as happy-go-lucky sellouts to the impoverished zine underground. Part of the genius of the early *MONDO* was the mix of edgy and playful content with an elegant expensive magazine design. It was Mu who insisted on the expensive glossy look and, together with the genius Art Dictator Bart Nagel, emphasized design. If it had been up to me, I'd still be in the garage hacking it out onto cheap newsprint.

The media attention was pretty extraordinary during this period from 1989-1992. And I discovered within myself a certain seductive eloquence that would emerge sort of automatically when I was in the presence of journalists. (Print journalists, mind you. I was *awful* on TV.) To be honest, I tried to hog as much publicity to myself as possible. If *MONDO* was to flame out, at least R.U. Sirius would have a career. I kept a close eye on incoming calls from the media, making sure to be the one to call them back, and insisted that the crew maintain a very complete and ready-to-be-sent media kit.

One reporter, Burr Snyder from the *San Francisco Chronicle,* came back to the *"MONDO* House" after a long lunch interview. As we were saying our goodbyes, John Barlow and Barbara Leary (Timothy's wife) showed up, they knew I had some DMT (the potent short acting hallucinogen) and they wanted to have some. Burr Snyder decided to join the fun. When we smoked, Barlow thought he was dead, and puked into a large pot. Snyder wrote, "The fun never stops. Spock it out kids. Put your eyes to the ether. As Einstein might put it, 'space-time's a-wastin'. *MONDO 2000* sez the future is *wow!"*

While I was mostly pleased with what journalists did when they covered *MONDO 2000,* I was troubled by reporters who would come around covering virtual reality and smart drugs, two areas that we covered in the magazine that were getting a lot of media hype at that time. These journalists composed their pieces as novelty items, and we were portrayed as *just too cute.* I didn't like to see the magazine's harder anarchic edges, or its genuine analytic insights, ignored. In fact, I disliked it so much that I started consistently emphasizing my ambiguities about these subjects in all interviews. But to no avail. They were there to portray us as VR-and-smart-drug advocating fruitcakes, so they would only include the one or two quotes that made us sound that way.

We covered so many issues and people during those years that would later crop up, primarily in *Wired*, but also all over the place. From encryption to virtual reality, from ATM hacking to digital music, we were on it in the early nineties. While the sorts of materials that now are covered more professionally but less enjoyably by *Wired* shaped *MONDO*'s popular image as way-out-in-front, it was the quirky stuff that made the magazine fun for me. Whether it was math genius Stephan Wolfram and superadvanced physicist Saul-Paul Sirag engaged in a way obscure conversation that nobody but they would understand or Queen Mu's strange tome on Jim Morrison's alleged penis cancer brought on by the use of tarantula venom, there was a surreal quality to *MONDO 2000* that drove people who take themselves too seriously to apoplexy. It was also, undoubtedly, a factor in convincing a technoculture elite that was a lot more conservative than the culture we were portraying that something a bit more like *Wired* was called for.

As with *High Frontiers,* I didn't do much writing in *MONDO.* I took my pleasure in shaping the overall vision of the magazine, and in pushing *MONDO* socially. I ended my thirties a "scenemaker." I had a hypersexy girlfriend and together we did too many drugs, went to all the parties and the early San Francisco raves, and made all kinds of connections. We were building our own dreams of multimedia potency as much as we were promoting *MONDO.* Ultimately these distractions would have almost zero payoff. I would spend most of the nineties jumping through hoops for projects that never came to fruition.

MONDO 2000 was the closest I ever came to something I consider a perfect situation; a group of people working together toward an ideal of scientific, technical, cultural, and political revolution, while at the same time being without dogma and completely irreverent, even towards our *selves*. The organization, or perhaps organism is a better word, was never comfortable or smooth. The internal workings at *MONDO* were chaotic, our existence always hanging by a thread. Public attention and expectation somehow made that reality seem all the more exasperating. At the end of 1992, with the completion and publication of my pet project, the M2k book, *MONDO 2000: A User's Guide to the New Edge,* I quit the magazine, dramatically walking out during an argument about the editorial value of Negativland's confrontation with U2's the Edge, a piece that I'd arranged.

It took me several years to realize that walking out on *MONDO* at that time was a big mistake. You gotta ride the wave you catch, because you may not catch another one. If I'd been stronger, more focused, less cocksure and ego-driven, more willing to fight for decisions I thought were important, and more patient about listening to the reasons for decisions that I disagreed with, *MONDO* might have kept its place as the lead magazine of technoculture and I might be rich, smug, and even more *exhausted* than I am.

Coming Out of Left Field: An Interview with Gracie & Zarkov

I didn't do a lot of writing for High Frontiers. *Hell, I didn't even do a lot of publishing. We came out with an issue a year. And what little writing I did was, in many ways, inferior to work I'd done in college. But it wasn't my writing, but the whole vibrant energy that came right off the pages of what the* SF Weekly *called a "party on paper" that made* High Frontiers *a special moment in countercultural history.*

This interview with the couple known as Gracie and Zarkov serves as a great example of the sort-of off-the-wall post-punk-neopsychedelic ranting that was High Frontiers *at its best. From the start, I really wanted to avoid—to whatever degree possible—the new age clichés that tend to crop up in psychedelic circles. The chance meeting with Gracie and Zarkov; sophisticated, scientific, urbane, eloquent, sexy,* weird *investment bankers—was a perfect example of the sort of dumb luck that I had while putting the thing together. Here was a couple doing crazed megadose hallucinatory drug experiments, writing out objective trip reports and distributing them, free, in a small xeroxed booklet called "Notes From the Underground." Who else but Gracie could talk about "invoking the goddess" without coming off like a bliss ninny?*

When I met them G&Z had just moved to Berkeley California from Chicago. They are still out here (in the Oakland Hills, actually), keeping together a low-key party scene (Great Friday night parties, but I'm just talking beer and junk food. Their drug trip sessions are infinitely more private affairs). Some of their writings can be found on the web at www.hyperreal.com

The following interview was published in two parts, in High Frontiers #2 and #3.

(with Lord Nose, *High Frontiers*, 1985)

Part One: lsd and mda (and little lambs eat ivy)

Zarkov and Gracie are two notorious acidheads with almost 20 years' experience in the areas of mythology, philosophy, psychoactive drugs, cosmology and irreverence. They currently fund their private researches by holding down jobs as investment bankers with large corporations. The results of these researches occasionally appear in self-published pamphlets under the general title "Notes from Underground." Recently, *High Frontiers* sponsored a gathering so that Gracie and Zarkov could indulge themselves in their favorite pastime... talking about these topics. Some of the more interesting and outlandish anecdotes appear below.

ZARKOV: The most unexpected and one of the weirdest experiences we've had was on mushrooms potentiated by harmala alkaloids. Based on the plant we used, we estimate that we had about 150-250 milligrams of mixed harmala alkaloids which we each took with 7.5 grams of dried stopharia cubensis mushrooms. It was an experience where the mushroon visions got brighter and brighter. Then, when I got to the point where they were unignorable, I was able to move around within the vision space. Finally, I entered into the vision itself, so that I was part of the vision. The interesting thing was that the characteristics of the vision were unchanged, the visions were still psilocybin visions. It was almost as if the harmala had provided a beautiful stage and lighting, built the auditorium, and then the mushroom provided the stage direction, plot and some of the characters.

The experience includes visions of about 50 or 60 different alien worlds, sometimes there was a soundtrack, sometimes there was a voice-over discussion and sometimes there was an argument that went along with the visions. I was free to move around in any particular world or I was free to, in effect, rip the curtain of the vision and walk through to another world. The trip was a series of vision after vision where I was trying to make direct contact with whatever was in charge of the visions.

On that particular trip I did not succeed in having a direct vision of the mushroom entities of a direct conversation with the voices that Terence (McKenna) talks about. However, on a succeeding trip, I did. I mean an experience of the literal, walk-right-into-your-living room, stand-there-and-look-at-you variety. Only when you look around, you aren't in your living room anymore.

Harmala alkaloids occur in several plants. For example, Sirian Rue, which, used in combination with psilocybin mushrooms, could have been the soma of the ancients. We've been doing some reading in Greek literature just this week and there seem to be references among the healing cults to the use of *Peganum Harmala* (Syrian Rue). The best known use of Harmala is in Yage or Ayahuasca in South America. Often it is used alone, but it seems that to get the most interesting visions, it is used with other tryptamines, primarily DMT-containing plants.

We are quite interested in this area of research and have additional Harmala experiments planned for the fall.

GRACIE: I had a similar experience on that combination in terms of choosing among a selection of visions. But what was interesting to me was that starting with that particular combination and with subsequent mushroom trips, we had our first fully-coupled trips. That is, we were getting exactly the same material at the same time. However, often we get it in different forms. For instance, I'll be seeing something and Zarkov will get the dialogue...

Z: ... or Gracie will hear a voice and I'll see something. The circumstances are usually a high-dose trip in a quiet darkened room with eyes closed. We will have the experience in a trance state and then we'll ask each other, "Well, what happened?" Then we'll find out it's the same material. Furthermore, it's like a serial. There is internal structure, a story. This is unlike LSD alone, which is kaleidoscopic. There is a sequential chain, start to finish, that is describable.

G: Now in the case we're talking about, the mushrooms were eaten first. The Harmala was a simple plant extract and it was smoked. I assume, because Yage is usually ingested as a boiled-water infusion (often with DMT admixtures), that the effects are different. It's probably more intense.

Z: Almost all of our far-out trips have been on combinations of psychedelics. One thing we have found is that the timing—that is the order you take the drugs in—

makes a dramatic difference. For example, the combination with which we have had the most experience is LSD combined with methoxylated amphetamines. There the timing is crucial, usually we start with MDA or MDMA. When the LSD is added, the trip is not so much different in form as it is in content. MDA alone gives you tremendous age regression capabilities. You start talking about your third birthday and things like that...

G: ... but add LSD and you get what you could call past lives, and false memory imagery. That is—imagery, feeling, or visions of being in another time, another place, or another personality.

Z: Using MDMA pretty much roots you firmly in the "now." It's also a little bit more other-directed, similar to "adam." In fact, many times people have equated adam with MMDA, somewhat incorrectly, since adam usually refers to MDM.

The MDA-LSD combination—in terms of synthetic combinations—have been the most consistent and controllable. Both Gracie and I have consistent series of personal visions, often times including the direct perception of—and discussion with—an entity we call the goddess.

The model we use is that the MDA, with its age-regression, including past lives, gives you all possibilities of all the people you were or could have been throughout history. Or it gives you the capability of being you in certain places back through history. The LSD, we always say, gives you the inside of your own head. It gives you all the possible potentialities of who you are or can be. When you take MDA and LSD simultaneously, you get a sort of matrix multiplication effect where you can observe yourself in all possible incarnations. In our case these have always seemed to be lineal ancestors. The Goddess entity sometimes explains the personal meaning of these visions to you directly.

G: For example, in my case I have used a trance technique with MDA and LSD to confront maternal programs. I got visions of how my mother treated me, how I reacted to my mother,, and had a full giving-birth-to-myself experience. The visions and ideational content were such that I could apply that information to fixing behavior that was obviously neurotic. Behaviors based on misunderstandings that developed at this particular point in my personal history.

Z: A technical note: we usually start with 100-300 micrograms of LSD. Upon feeling the first effects, we take 75-125 milligrams of MDA. Since MDA is often cut, this refers to pure MDA. The MDA-LSD combination structures the personal information that you often get fleeting glimpses of on LSD alone. The MDA makes it directly personal and puts it into a context that you can relate to.

The testability of all this strange stuff is "can you use it?" We've never gotten voices raving, saying "You were the high priest of Atlantis." It's fairly mundane and believable. Yet, when it's information about yourself or your friends, it's psychological and behavioral insights that you had been unable to obtain otherwise. By putting these insights or directions, so to speak, into action, they work! I mean they work in the everyday world. You apply these insights by behaving that way to your friends and the specific problems that you were having disappear and you are a happier human being.

G: It's (MDA-LSD) an oracular sort of approach. You develop your mind set and setting—you ask the question, about the problem you are trying to solve. Then you can go in seeking whatever deity or entity will show up to give you information or show you useful answers.

Z: Our familiarity with MDA came about via a picaresque route. We used to be associated with a variety of sex clubs. One of the most popular drug combinations at parties was MDA and speed or MDA and cocaine.

G: MDA and cocaine, a terrible combination! Blah! What you get is the friendliest dinosaur you ever saw in your life. You take this Tyrannosaurus Rex and make him cuddly and erotic and you've got the idea. I remember a scene involving someone in a monocle, a white silk scarf, a nazi helmet and a cockring... truly bizarre.

Z: MDA can make you feel erotic. The neurophysical side effects of MDA are similar to the neurophysical effects of sexual arousal. It also causes, particularly in women, water retention, especially in the breasts and buttocks. It's also a drug that confuses you enough so that when your body says... "Well, physically I feel like I feel when I'm turned on..." Your mind replies, "I must be turned on." At the same time, it makes everything, especially other people, appear much more beautiful, so if you're in a sexual setting, like a sex party the results can be amazing. The first time I witnessed the mass consumption of MDA at a sex party, a usually relatively shy woman stood up and said, "There are six horny, hopped-up women in the hot tub and we hope there are some men who want to fuck us!" to lead the party off. That sort of behavior in the right setting is not atypical of MDA and uppers.

One warning, however. All methoxylated amphetamines—MDA, MDM, MMDA, etc.— are fairly poisonous, depending on who you believe and which drug. The lethal dose is between 500-1600 milligrams. There is also considerable individual variation, so be careful!

One of the things that we have found is that the more psychedelic each substance is by itself, the more interesting the effects when you combine them. When you get to some of the later Shulgin drugs that are more specific in terms of action, these drugs become less interesting. At least to us, we would like the widest range of effects that we have a chance of controlling.

G: I talked before about developing your set and setting. We used a variety of self-developed rituals to modify the setting. We use music; I use dance a lot. It's a question of personal preference. Since we both have strong musical backgrounds, we've used music to structure trips or to provide a framework within which the more profound effects can take place. It can be used as a control if things get particularly freaky of wild. My dancing grows out of the drugs and the music. In my case dancing is a way of conjuring up entities, of using it as a way of putting myself in an altered state of consciousness on top of the drug or in addition to the drug to produce a predictable possession or entity-contacting-type effects.

We also use sex. The sex is partly because of the accident, or synchronicity of our being in the sex business for awhile. Also we found that many of the explicitly tantric techniques are effective in the same way as the music or the dance, not only for controlling a trip but for sending it in a specific direction or getting higher so that you get more profound effects from the drugs.

Another option that we would recommend is to make up your own religion. We use a modification of a goddess-type religion.

Part Two: Coming Out of Left Field

Our resident designer heads, Gracie and Zarkov, continue their aleotonic journey through mythology, philosophy, epistemology, psychedelic drugs and irreverence.

GRACIE: We first ran into Goddess imagery when I was doing manifestation or possession states. Not possession in the sense of blacking out, but possession in the sense of being in contact with an entity who was expressed through dance or facial expressions or unusual turns of phrase or changes in voice.

ZARKOV: A couple of times these were actually extended raps that Gracie could give.

G: Right, but without losing my sense of personal ego. I was still Gracie, but at the same time I was Circe or Aphrodite or whoever.

HIGH FRONTIERS: Which Goddess was it?

G: It varied. Aphrodite, Hecate, Athena... eventually we got back to a sort of Sumerian, but sort of generalized...

Z: Goddess of Sex, Goddess of Love, Goddess of Procreation, fertility, definitely agriculture, definitely war... so it sort of fits the Innana complex.

G: When asked during a contact, they all tended to call themselves "The Goddess," and I am emphasizing the capital letters. That's their terminology.

HF: Does all this arise from psychedelic experience?

Z: We have not been able to make definite contact except in altered states. The interesting thing to us is that we didn't get The Goddess on the tryptamines (until our recent betacarboline experiments), although we know of a person who's had quite a bit of experience with psychedelic states who recently has gotten her own particular version of The Goddess on mushrooms.

My first encounter with The Goddess was the first real contact experience I'd had. I've had contact with about out a half dozen different entities since then on various occasions—but what makes this so impressive was that I wasn't a believer in these types of phenomena on a gut level. What I got on that particular contact was very specific advice on how to deal with people in my life. Basically, I was having personal difficulty with certain people who are close to me, when we were just beginning exploratory combinations of MDA and LSD. I fell into a trance, got into contact, and The Goddess started a rap. It was a lengthy set of situation-specific pieces of advice on how to behave. Now, what was strange was that much of the voice I couldn't understand at the time. The characteristics of The Goddess singing were like fast tape-recorder music, like someone singing too fast to understand. Tonally, it was beautiful. It didn't sound like Minnie Mouse. At the end of the contact, I was symbolically given golden scrolls, and for about six months after the contact, when I ended up in a situation with the people I was troubled about, I would hear a brief burst of this singing, and sometimes I would see in my mind's eye the scroll—and what was strange was that now I understood the advice. Several people commented that all of a sudden I was much easier to get along with. I was paying more attention to their needs, or whatever. I thought, this is pretty strange. There's no way I could tell them why. They'd think I'd absolutely lost it.

Another type of psychedelic experience that we clearly try to distinguish from "contact" is where we will have strange trains of thought or borderline visions where the archetypes come out and play around, perhaps the great God Pan, Hera, Innana, Ishtar... but you've not got a clear case of an entity sitting down on the beanbag chair next to you and giving you a rap, but all of a sudden you have an understanding, or a thought that wasn't in your head before... that you can identify with the archetypes.

G: Or facial changes that we see in each other. That's one of the other ways of using sex magic—you can, while fucking, look at each other and watch faces change. We've had the Pan entity show up.

HF: How'd you do it?

Z: If you want to go into a trance, usually the best way is MDA, first, 100-150 milligrams, then LSD about 150-200 micrograms about a half hour later. The other way is a moderate dose of LSD—moderate meaning 150-200 micrograms—enough to definitely be high, and then anywhere from 3 to 4 hours later, a fairly high dose of MDA, 120-200 milligrams, and then play these sorts of games, e.g. sex magic, ritual, etc.

G: The mescaline-LSD mix—we used mescaline first followed by LSD—can provide tremendous insights into psychological states, into neurotic ways of thinking, and can help you blow those right out of the water. The mescaline LSD mix is particularly interesting because it seems to bring some of your neurotic programs right up front where you can see them working. It brings it up on the screen and shows you just what that strange loop is, just what that incorrect thought is.

If you're always doing the same drug at the same dose in the same setting repeatedly, you're probably not getting anywhere. And we've found that one of the best ways to make sure you keep making progress is to vary things. Vary the substances you use, vary the dosage, vary your set, vary your setting. If you always do it outdoors, do it inside in the dark for a change. If you always do it in the dark, go outside and do it.

Read. Between your trips pick a particular topic that you want to study—something you're going to work on, a particular historical period that interest you, a particular issue in art or music, and spend the whole week studying that. For example, say you want to explore body language and representation of the body. Read *The Nude in Art*, read *Seeing Through Clothes*, do some mirror meditation with your own body, do some yoga, do all those things the week before and then trip and do body-oriented things and talk about it. You get much more material that just saying "I want to have a body-oriented trip" and taking some drugs.

Z: We argue continually about the purpose of psychedelics. But I think our position right now is that it beats bowling. It's very interesting to do. It's a form of research. What can you say about substances that ask "How would you like to see travelogues of a planet 13 light years away?" and you go "Why not?" and you see visions of sea

91

serpents that turn into beautiful naked women, and back into sea serpents. The voice then says, "You know, you should think about that, there's a message there for you," and you go "Well, OK." It beats worrying about whether the Reagan tax package is going to pass.

G: You get a lot of insights into any area of study. Noetic anthropology is the term we use, which I think is borrowed from Terence. Sometimes we try to figure out just how to get into the heads of the people who were around in pre-dynastic Egypt. Or just what was going on in Minoan civilization? Trying to figure out what was going on back there, especially since much of the historical material is difficult to interpret because we're living in a post-patriarchal culture, is of interest.

Z: The edge of pre-history to history, as to what really happened…

G: …. is an area that interests us particularly because we think it speaks very specifically to the human dilemma in modern times. That is, "What do we—as a species and individuals—do now?" One of the most important things we think we do—and certainly we do it for each other—is to inspire optimism and a sense of purpose. I think there's a widespread feeling of despair, of not being able to do anything about the destiny of the human race. I think it's important more and more to psyche ourselves up to think in a heroic sort of way about what action each individual can take. I think these kinds of studies—including the work on your own head, including the work on periods in history—are absolutely essential to understanding ourselves. And understanding yourself is the single most important step anyone can take in terms of maximizing the likelihood of the human race not only surviving, but moving on to a better kind of existence.

HF: Do you identify the patriarchal stage with scarcity consciousness?

G: That notion plugs into something we've been talking about recently that is based on John Pfeiffer, the paleoanthropologist, and his book on prehistoric cave art, *The Creative Explosion*. He talks about the transition from an early hunter-gatherer prehistoric period in which, for tens of thousands of years, during the early development of the human race, the species evolved under conditions so different from what we have now that it's very hard for us to imagine being those kinds of people. Living where game was so abundant, where gathering things to eat was so easy that there was an enormous population growth, which has resulted in a fight against scarcity ever since.

Z: We're talking tens of thousands of years.

G: But I think that 8-10,000 years is what is normally considered the start of the patriarchal period. And I think that it was in response to that feeling of wanting to wrest control because you could no longer count on the Goddess to pour out her abundance for you with very little effort. Perhaps after the move to space, we'll be able to enter a period of unlimited resources where we can get back to that kind of "normal" human psychology which we haven't seen for 10-15,000 years. And in that sense, I'd have to say that we've got a goal.

HF: What is your impression of the sort of hardware/software argument about moving into space? The hardware as the sort of masculine Western roadtrip and the software is… well, some people carry the argument as far as to say that we can move there spiritually of psychically, perhaps even rather than physically.

G: The issue of hardware and software, like the issue of male and female, black and white, day and night, is the old dualistic bugaboo that has been plaguing most of humanity one way or another for a long time. And I think we've got to get past it. I think that we are both our hardware and our software. Right now our hardware dies, and that's a real limitation we're stuck with. When we figure out how to make the hardware immortal, that'll solve the hardware problem. On the software question— we don't know what happens to the software when the hardware dies. Does the software go somewhere else? We don't know where that somewhere else might be. Is there a way to separate the hardware from the software so it doesn't matter if the hardware dies?

Z: There's a lot more information "out there" than has physical reality, and it just so happens that there are things that occur physically like this glass. But there are a lot more things "out there" of all kinds and shapes that probably aren't made out of silicon dioxide like this glass, or carbon and water like we are.

What you see on psychedelics—you just don't know whether it exists or not. One of the strangest trips so far put me on this other planet subjectively for three days. Objectively for 4 hours. But on that planet the sun came up, I got warm. The sun went down, I got cold. I could swim. I could eat. I could make love to the inhabitants. I looked at my boots, the details were there—I mean, I was *there*. I've never had a vision like that before—it's always movies on the eyelids.

G: I would certainly be in agreement with Leary and Wilson and other people who emphasize life extension, that we should get the hardware to work as well as possible and as long as possible because right now it's the most powerful tool we have for manipulating what we perceive as reality. Somehow I have an intuition—although it's only an intuition and not something I would try to claim as true—that there's something very important about being embodied. That's a very real problem for us as conscious entities to solve. Why be embodied? And why is embodiment such a temporary, painful, and sloppy sort of solution?

HF: Do you think some people, on psychedelics, might be grinding their neuroses in even deeper?

Z: Definitely. That's a real good point.

G: I think that's especially easy to do with LSD if you believe that it loosens your imprints and conditioning and allows you to re-imprint and recondition. If you re-imprint and recondition with the same stuff that you had when you began, you reinforce whatever neurotic programs you already have.

HF: Do you think psychedelics should be used by a large number of people—that it's necessary in order to move in time and space and eliminate the neurosis in humans? How many people should do it? Antennae for the species?

Z: Number one, as thorough-going libertarians, we believe they shouldn't be regulated. Period. But personally, I do not recommend, particularly given most people's education and personalities, that large numbers of people take psychedelics. On the other hand, I don't think there's an elite, an elite priesthood, no matter how it's defined. Being generally against authority, the last thing in the world I want is anybody getting control of who does and who does not use these drugs. That's worse than having them illegal. The use of these drugs should be an individual's independent and thoughtful choice.

We live encased in a lot of delusions. Many of these delusions could have foundations that date back to pre-history. One advantage psychedelics allow you, if you pursue them with any kind of care, is the ability to move outside the local delusions to try to see alternatives. For example, we may be able to put off a major war on this planet for a few more years, but 100% prevention forever of nuclear war, given current thoughts and current circumstances, is unlikely. Something has to change. Many people who are involved in space and computers, whether it be financing or technology, do psychedelics for inspiration. Some of the inspirations provide reasons for space migration—one could be escape, one could be shifting the world scarcity equation to make peace more probable.

More deeply than that, you can make significant repairs to your head, you can become a happier human being, you can become healthier, you can become less deluded, you can become more effective and make a stronger contribution in the real world using these drugs. Leary said that everyone who is on the leading edge in any of these things has to come to terms with psychedelics in some fashion. That's certainly true...

Z: Our current science is the outcome of the Western heresy that individuals can understand the universe. We have culturally let science be taken over by a bunch of reductionist technicians. The great scientists of the recent past—at the beginning of the century—would have very little to do with the reductionist philosophy.

G: It's only really in the last 25 years that new models, new mathematics, new ways of describing the universe in the abstract have developed that might do a better job. Like catastrophe theory, fractal mathematics, Prigogine's theories of dissipative structures, etc.

Science, in the classical sense, is now very much in the position that the Church was in the 16th Century—as "The Model" that would describe everything, the motion of the planets, how living systems work, how to be an ethical person, etc. We don't so much need a new model or a new paradigm as a whole bunch of new models and new paradigms, and to learn ways to apply those to the domains where they fit best.

Z: That's what we mean by science, hard Baconian facts. It should be pure empiricism. You give DMT to ten people. They never had DMT before, and you tell them only that they might see something. If nine out of ten of them come back with descriptions of elves, and four of them use the word elves unprompted, we think you should investigate the phenomenon of elves seen on DMT. Twentieth Century research into the mind is about as advanced as Lavoisier's chemistry in the eighteenth century.

G: Coming out of left field is the thought we'd probably like to leave you with. There's a lot of research in numerous fields. Intelligent people are working on all sorts of problems. No one knows where the next answers will come from. I think fewer come from a society that says you should limit what you think about to these dozens or so topics that are socially acceptable. You're more likely to get better solutions to more problems in an atmosphere that maximizes the freedom of individuals to choose whatever topics they're interested in, and to follow that interest as deeply and as thoroughly and as weirdly as they feel is necessary.

Z: I'll close with a quote from one of my favorite people, Socrates. He said. "The unexamined life is not worth living." What else is there to say?

And we've chosen to close with a passage from paleoanthropologist John Pfeiffer's recent book *The Creative Explosion:*

"Think of the hundreds of thousands of useless things that are going on in the world somewhere right now. There seems to be no limit to what people will do, provided that it is sufficiently offbeat, and has never been done before. All the new games and experiments and assorted forms of dare-deviltry, everything from double somersault ski-jumps, walking tightropes between skyscrapers, and setting the record for the most parachute jumps in a 24-hour period, to wrapping cliffs in cellophane, swallowing new drugs or combinations of drugs, playing Dungeons and Dragons, attempts at levitation, and on and on and on. Such activities represent the cutting edge of evolution, human-style. They are analogous to the random genetic mutations of organic evolution. The vast majority of mutations are harmful or useless, and so are the vast majority of offbeat activities. But someday as society changes at a mounting rate, one in a billion may pay off, and it's impossible to predict which one.

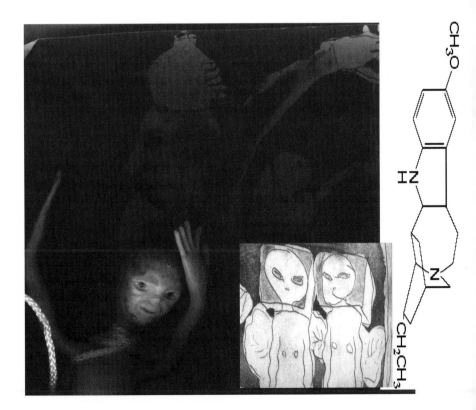

The CIA, LSD and the Occult: an Interview with Martin Lee

While Jeff Mark and I did the interview, this elegant introduction could only be the work of Queen Mu.

with Severe Tire Damage, *High Frontiers*, 1987

Martin A. Lee is the author, with Bruce Schlain, of the best-selling book, *Acid Dreams*. Here he talks to *High Frontiers* about some of the bits he left out of the book. In a recent telephone conversation, Marty continues to speculate—on the connection between Italian Fascist philosopher Julius Evola with his "spiritual warrior elite," Rene Guenon (the French esotericist) and mescaline; on the reported fascination with psychedelics by Sartre, Maurice Merleau-Ponti and Henri Michaux. The links are intriguing if difficult to pin down. Clearly though, by the 1930s, an awareness of hallucinogens had spread through artistic and literary circles in Berlin and other European capitals. Founded on the German Romantic fascination with deliriants like henbane, it was fueled by Lewis Lewin's *Phantastica* and Kurt Beringer's *Der Mescalinrausch* (1927). German Expressionist poet-physician Gottfried Benn described the "cerebral oscillations" produced by alkaloids in "Provoked Life: The Anthropology of the Ego." Klee, Kluver, Hesse, and Jung round out the list of luminaries who reportedly dabbled in hallucinogens.

All this merely contextualizes the really heavy-duty experimentation with psychedelics which Joseph Borkin stumbled on in researching *The Crime and Passion of I.G. Farben*. A discovery which Borkin left out of the book was that I.G. Farben maintained, throughout the '30s, a special secret division devoted to research on psychotomimetic agents. In *Acid Dreams*, Martin Lee detailed the Nazi mind control experiments with mescaline carried out by Nazi doctors at Dachau. Here he raises the interesting point that LSD, first synthesized in 1938, actually fell into the ambit of I.G. Farben when they gobbled up Sandoz that same year. Curiouser and curiouser!

And what about the occult bureau within the Third Reich called the Ahnwerbe? And the secret societies operating within our own industrial and intelligence communities? Read on!

This interview was conducted by R.U. Sirius and Severe Tire Damage in a greasy diner in San Francisco.

HIGH FRONTIERS: Your book brought to mind *The Seven Faces of Dr. Lao*. It was like an allegory about human folly. LSD is the mysterious stranger who comes to town and everybody relates to him in their own strange way. They all get to manifest their character flaws and their positive traits in an intensified way through their interaction with him. I thought that, of all the characters in your book, LSD came off the most admirably. In doing the book, what did you learn about the nature of reality and about human beings?

MARTIN LEE: It showed me that humans have a fantastic capacity for self-deception. As for the mystical implications of the LSD experience, I wouldn't want people who read the book to come away with the idea that those people who thought it was a sacrament got it wrong. And I wouldn't want them to come away thinking that the perception of the infinite is beyond the grasp or is not the business of people in general. I would suggest quite the opposite. The drug, in and of itself, may not be a sacrament, but it *does* produce mystical experiences. I'd say that these experiences aren't inherent in the drug, they're inherent in ourselves. If it's an ecstatic drug, it is because we are capable of experiencing ecstasy. If it's an insightful drug, it is because we have insights waiting to be born. And if it yields mystical perceptions, it is because we have that potential for mystical perceptions. So, if anything, it reaffirms something very basic about human nature which cuts across all cultures and all times and that should not be beyond the grasp of people. It should be everybody's birthright to have those kinds of experiences and perceptions. This, of course, does not necessarily require a drug. But LSD certainly makes it easier or quicker. So I don't want people to come away thinking that the people who had profound mystical experiences got it all wrong. On the other hand, I wouldn't want people to think that the CIA got it wrong in seeing LSD as an anxiety-producing drug.

I came away from your book with this thought; when people try to put their own stamp on the psychedelic experience and use it either as a tool or a weapon, it becomes problematic. It's too unpredictable and doesn't conform to human goals, however noble.

I can easily understand how people like Leary can assume that, because they've had these incredible experiences, that the experiences are inherent in the drug and everyone else will have similar experiences. They were mistakenly attributing the experience to the drug rather than their own minds. Once you start thinking that way, the idea becomes to make this available to as many people as possible and then they will automatically share certain perceptions that will be interesting, insightful, helpful, positive perceptions. Things can only get better. I can understand how people could get into something like that, particularly when they had television and other mass media at their disposal. Not only did they have this substance that seemed to be guaranteed to produce a certain kind of positive experience but they also had the media at their beck and call. So they could get the message across just like that.

It was the combination of these factors... for the first time in human history, you have massive amounts, millions of doses of a hallucinogen (a synthetic hallucinogen which is effective in minute amounts so that the potential supply is virtually unlimited, whereas previously you had only natural hallucinogens) and also for the first time you have social movements interacting with this powerful new perceptual technology, television, in a way that has no precedent for the species. So you have these two powerful perceptual technologies intersecting, colliding with social movements. It created a situation which was so interesting and full of promise that people did not realize the pitfalls. Maybe on the next go-around they will not make the same mistakes.

What made you want to begin research in this subject?

I had participated somewhat as an "activist" at the tail end of the '60s and I identified strongly with both the political and cultural upheavals of that time to the extent that one can appreciate such matters at fourteen. I had an inherent interest in terms of this being my background or roots. So part of it was trying to understand something about me and something about the culture that would shed light on something about me. It's historical and personal. I had a personal interest in understanding this. In terms of the CIA stuff, that grows from literary and journalistic interests.

Did that interest arise after the Church Committee as a result of the public testimony that went on there?

A little bit before. I was interested in the Kennedy assassination. With some friends, I was working on a group called the Assassination Information Bureau. It was a legitimate, albeit poorly-funded, grass roots group. We did some good work there against all odds. While we were down in Washington, everyone got into areas that seemed related to the question of the Kennedy assassination. And I got into drug testing, mind control, initially thinking this would throw light on the whole assassination question. Mafia plots against Castro, things like that. Eventually I got much more interested in understanding what was happening with the CIA and drugs.

Very early on, I postulated the question, what is the relationship between the subterranean CIA business and the counterculture sixties stuff? I had a hunch that there was some kind of relationship and, by studying it, I might throw some light on what happened in the '60s. I wasn't thinking that there was some grand conspiracy where the CIA manipulated everything, but just thinking that there was an important relationship there.

You've been making it very clear in your lectures that your investigation of the whole relationship of the CIA to the psychedelic explosion has *not* led you to conclude that the CIA was behind it all but rather that the cat got out of the bag and then, once it did, the CIA did their best to keep an eye on it, control it, manipulate it... do all the things you'd expect spooks to do. But a lot of the people who read the book come away thinking that the whole psychedelic counterculture thing was just a CIA plot. Some conspiracy freaks are even saying that Leary was CIA.

That's terrible. I spent a lot of time talking to Tim and I really like him. In some ways the CIA was like an unwitting midwife in the birth of the acid generation. Leary himself likes to say that the CIA started everything but that's just a touch of Learyesque hyperbole.

As I see the picture, you have certain streams feeding into what is going to be the roaring river of the sixties upheavals, and one of these streams is the CIA/army experiments. That overlaps with the scientific research community, mostly the psychotomimetic school. Then there are the legitimate overground researchers who are more of the psychedelic school, and that overlaps with the literary circles, Huxley and so forth, and the Beats to some degree. The Beats form almost a third stream. It is a commingling of all these different streams that sets the stage for what happens. Granted, there are certain obvious sociological factors that make it a very ripe and fertile setting.

Did you ever suspect the possibility of there being some secret society, perhaps having some occult or magical purposes, manipulating the whole thing—the CIA, the acid... did you bump into anything in this area?

I did! And I didn't put any of this into my book, but I'll tell you. I have done research on secret societies and regarding the Catholic Church, the Knights of Malta, I broke the story a few years ago about the CIA and the Knights of Malta. They are a very old order going back to the crusades, Freemasonry and that sort of thing. These secret societies do play a far greater role in history than most historians acknowledge.

First of all, everyone knows the Nazis were very much into the occult. There are rumors that Hitler experimented with peyote. We know that the Nazis experimented with mescaline at Dachau. Now consider that Hitler's inner circle was very much involved with the occult. They had an occult bureau within the SS called the Ahnwerbe. They were interested in the Tibetan stuff, interested in pre-Christian, Gnostic Greek pagan-oriented matters. These people appear to have been open-minded and receptive to the notion of altered states. The Nazis were really uptight about the Freemasons and tried to crack down on them—they were aware enough to sense the power there.

For the LSD story, Allan Dulles was in Switzerland during the war; at one point he was joined in Switzerland by Carl Jung, who had been in Germany up until 1942 as editor of *Zentralblatt Für Psychoterapie,* perhaps, the pre-eminent psychiatric journal. This was when Jung, instead of talking about the collective unconscious, started taking about the racial unconscious and how Jewish archetypes were different from other archetypes. He started getting into some of that stuff. (I think there was a sleazy side of Jung, although he is an amazing figure, don't get me wrong. But there was a strange side to him that people like to forget.)

Jung worked with Dulles giving psychological assessments of Nazi leaders and giving that information to the OSS. There is reason to believe Jung experimented with Peyote. He certainly was aware of such substances and had written about them and referred to them in certain contexts. I don't know if he had personal contact. It's quite possible Jung may have imparted to Dulles certain information about these chemicals, and it is under Dulles that the LSD stuff begins happening in a big way in the CIA. Dulles' assistant in Switzerland was Ann Bancroft, who was Jung's chief student at the time. (She has written a book, *Autobiography of a Spy,* published by Morrow.)

Something that I've given some thought to as far as the LSD story goes is this gap in time from 1938, when Dr. Hofmann first synthesized it, to 1943 when he discovered its effects. Before I go into this, let me put it into context. I have no reason to doubt Dr. Hofmann's honesty or his story about how LSD was discovered. I hope to talk to Hofmann in Europe. We are really lucky to have him. A great guy. Such vitality. He is really one of the best advertisements for his product.

Nevertheless, there are some curious things that came up that I can't help but wonder about. One point of interest is that during the time when he made that discovery, Sandoz was linked, through cartel agreements, to I.G. Farben Chemical, which was the largest chemical company in the world and was really the backbone of the whole Third Reich war effort. I.G. Farben had extensive links with American pharmaceutical corporations. The legal aspect of that link was represented by Sullivan and Cromwell which was the law firm Allen Dulles worked for. Dulles was in Switzerland not only as a spy but also as a businessman who was still continuing those links through secret associations between American corporations and the Nazis, which was all illegal and hush hush during the war.

I.G. Farben was so dominant during the war that they gobbled up everybody. Sandoz was a sitting duck. Generally speaking, the way it would work is I.G. Farben entered into these agreements whereby they would have automatic patent rights to any new invention or discovery made by those corporations that were gobbled up by them through these cartel links. Therefore, should that apply to Sandoz, as I have very reason to believe it did from my study of how I.G. Farben operated, it would mean that at the time Hofmann synthesized LSD, technically speaking, that would have been the property of I.G. Farben, this monster corporation that was running some of the concentration camps and slave labor at Auschwitz, bad news business. What if Hofmann really knew all along what it was, or somebody else did?

Again, I'll put this into context. I don't believe that he is lying. But it is curious. It could certainly have been an accident, as Dr. Hofmann says. But on the other hand, even if the effects of the stuff went unrecognized until 1943, even then, technically speaking, through the patent agreements, it should've gone to I.G. Farben at a time when they were testing mescaline at Dachau. We can be certain that the Nazi high command was already aware of these substances. They do not just go testing such things without those very high up knowing about it and giving the orders.

Imagine if the Nazis had LSD? Or maybe Hofmann and company withheld the discovery for political reasons. The patent wasn't filed until 1946, three years after the supposed discovery of the effects. By then, the Third Reich had collapsed.

That is one story. There is another story that I did not put in my book. According to Captain Al Hubbard, Hofmann did not discover it in 1943, nor in '38, but much earlier. (Captain Alfred M. Hubbard was the spy who became the first Johnny Appleseed of LSD.) According to Hubbard, Hofmann was part of a small group of people who were nominally connected with Steiner's anthroposophy group in the early '30s and they systematically decided and set out to make a peace pill to help mankind. They saw the beginnings of the Nazi emergence, so they consciously set out to make something like LSD, which they did and then kept it secret from the world.

Now there is absolutely no evidence to confirm that, and Captain Al Hubbard is an exaggerator. Hubbard is an aggrandizer. He likes to be the one who knows. That's his character. But it's a curious story and I would not completely discount it. Hubbard knows a lot of things. The basic outline of one rather wild story he told a friend of mine proved correct, although some of the details may be exaggerated. This particular talk, I could not confirm.

Regarding secret societies—well, when you come down to it, the CIA *is* a secret society. And within the CIA, there are all kinds of secret societies operating. The Freemasons are in the CIA. The Knights of Malta are in the CIA, and other groups. These different secret societies are not just within the CIA but in the corporate world, the Joint Chiefs of Staff, the FBI, the Defense Department, etceteras. These societies, if we understood them, might help delineate certain factions within the power elite.

I think it works on two levels. For the proletariat—for the rest of us—the Rotary,

Masonry, doesn't really mean anything. But at the very highest levels, then you're dealing with very influential and powerful individuals . . . at that level, perhaps studying these different groups can shed some light on understanding different factions within the ruling elite.

I don't think that these groups represent vital mystical bodies or traditions. I think they're decrepit. They're like organized religion and don't represent a real mystical current anymore. They're fossilized structures.

I can imagine that if these groups had any mystical underpinnings and suddenly they're dosed with LSD, they might think... MY GOD! We've got the ultimate key to power now! That might have played a part in their enthusiasm for it.

My sense is that these societies have nothing to do with their original mystical roots. So in that sense they're not guarding mystical secrets. It's more like the secret machinations of the power elite. When you get to that level of power you know plenty of secrets but I don't think it has anything to do with the secrets of the mystical roots of Masonry. Now, certainly Masons are not supposed to reveal the rituals they go through. They lie in coffins with bandannas around their eyes, with pictures of severed limbs and heads dripping blood. But I think, at this point, it's mostly male bonding and such.

So, after all of this, what do you think about LSD? Do you have an existential or epistemological overview of what it's all about?

I'm aware that these views exist. I'm aware that people like Terence McKenna and Timothy Leary and so on, have various models to explain these experiences.

Experience is concrete. One derives different metaphors, scientific or whatnot, to shed light on that basic experience. I don't have much way of responding to those theories. During this kind of social history research, I came to be hesitant to ascribe anything to LSD itself. I came away from it with a healthy respect for ambiguity and not knowing it all.

Is There Any Escape From Stupid?

An Interview with Negativland by Stephan Ronan
and R.U. Sirius

In the mid-80s, High Frontiers *sponsored a "Reality Hackers Forum" at a small auditorium in Berkeley called the Julia Morgan Center. Once a month, we'd have somebody lecture about something obscure; Terence McKenna and quantum physicist Nick Herbert talked about time travel, Rudy Rucker talked about cyberpunk (in 1988), Ted Nelson talked about Project Xanadu (the philosophy underpinning hypercard, hypermedia, and the world wide web). After an hour long talk, we would break and then have an open public discussion about... well... reality hacking. What could we do to reprogram the sick sad world? A couple of the more radical and outspoken participants in these discussions were Mark Hosler and Don Joyce. They were members of a very funny sound-collage art band called Negativland and Don hosted the brilliant sound collage show "Over The Edge" on Berkeley's KPFA.*

In 1988, Negativland was in the media, after committing their first of a series of very subversive, very successful, and in some ways very self-destructive pranks. Interviewing them for an early issue of MONDO 2000 was a natural. Freelance art/beat literature historian, writer, and occasional "Over the Edge" collaborator Stephan Ronan joined me in this conversation with Mark Hosler and Don Joyce.

Three years, and many MONDOs later, I would somewhat famously involve MONDO with Negativland in a bit of guerrilla journalism. Negativland had just been sued by Island Records for its audio collage commentary on—among other things—that record label's most popular band, U2. This Negativland CD, called U2, *was pulled from circulation and the band had to pay $90,000 to Island, the equivalent of about a penny within the music industry, but enough to put the Negativland members in the poor house.*

So when, by coincidence, U2's representative phoned up MONDO offering an interview with The Edge about the band's use of technology—and the cyberpunk overtones—of their Zoo TV show, I accepted. I got in touch with Mark and Don and had them laying in wait when Edge phoned up from Dublin.

The resulting dialogue was more Negativland diatribe. They ranted at the flustered rock star, who had already confessed to the sin of appropriating found media from cable television without permission during the Zoo TV tour. The interview ends with Hosler asking Edge for a loan, as Edge howls with laughter, and declares the experience "the most surrealistic interview I've ever done."

The funny thing is, while it was a great act of cultural subversion, it was not *a great interview, so Queen Mu wanted to shorten it up substantially. I got all hotheaded and quit the magazine over this. In retrospect, Mu may have been right. It was the act and not the interview that was successful and a shortened version might have communicated just as well. In fact, I choose not to include it in this book, in deference to the quality of this earlier piece.*

Negativland is without a doubt the most peculiar presence on College radio's alternative music play lists. They might be described as an industrial/media/humor band, but then again some of their stuff is so peculiar that even that description sounds too self-consciously arty. Whatever, they are definitely not a rock band.

The following chronology (printed here almost in its entirety) came with the latest Negativland record, *Helter Stupid* and is required reading if you're to understand the interview that follows.

• 10/20/87 Negativland releases their fourth album, *Escape from Noise* and begin preparation for a national tour. The album includes the cut "Christianity is Stupid," which features the "found" vocals of Reverend Estes Pirkle from a sermon recorded in 1968.

• 2/20/88 Story appears in the *New York Times,* national wire services, and radio and TV network news relating the arrest of sixteen-year-old David Drom in the ax murder of his father, mother, sister and brother two days earlier in Rochester, Minnesota. The *NY Times* article mentions that David and his father had argued over a music tape David had listened to. The Brom's are described as a devout Roman Catholic family.

• 3/10/88 Negativland cancels the tour when it becomes apparent that it will lose money. The group decides to send their American label, SST Records, a phony press release for distribution which attributes the cancellation of the tour to pressure from "Federal Officer Dick Jordan" who had advised the band not to leave town pending the investigation of the Brom murders. The press release implies that David and his parents had been arguing about Negativland's song "Christianity is Stupid" just prior to the murders. The *NY Times* article is distributed with the press release.

• 3/16/88 Negativland receives phone call from *Rockpool, Pulse, BAM* magazine, and several other fanzines requesting more information about the link between Negativland and the Brom murders. The group maintains that the federal interference is indeed real, but declines to elaborate.

• 3/30/88 In Minnesota, Judge Gerrard Ring "gags" media coverage of the David Brom case, pending his decision as to whether David will be tried as a juvenile or an adult. After entering no plea in a pre-trial hearing, David Brom undergoes a series of forensic psychiatric tests.

• 4/20/88 Citing federal restraints against participating in any live promotion dealing with the Brom case, Negativland consents to a phone interview with *BAM* magazine. When pressed for information by interviewer Steve Stolder, a group member mentions a "bloody cassette tape" in passing.

• 4/22/88 Judge Ring rules that David Brom be tried as a juvenile. The prosecution appeals.

• 5/6/88 *BAM* prints a full-page article on Negativland and the Brom case by Steve Stolder, despite Stolder's inability to establish the existence of "Federal Authority Dick Jordan" and despite Stolder's phone conversation with James Walsh, the *Rochester Post Bulletin* reporter assigned to the Brom case. In several months of covering the story, Walsh has never heard of Negativland. The article simply restates the "facts" from the Negativland press release with no trace of skepticism.

• 5/9/88 James Walsh contacts SST Records, requesting more information on the Negativland-Brom connection. SST sends him a copy of the original press release and puts Walsh in contact with the group. Negativland declines to do more than restate the "rumor" that "Christianity is Stupid" may have caused an argument among the Brom's that precipitated the murders. Negativland now begins to draw back from direct stimulation of the media by claiming that a phony lawyer, Hal Stakke, had advised them not to discuss the case with anyone.

• ?/?/88 Negativland hires a press clipping service to gather copies of all articles pertaining to the Brom case. Articles on Negativland mentioning the Brom link eventually appeared in *Rockpool, Boston Rock, Buttrag, Pulse, San Francisco Chronicle, Pollstar, Cut, Spy Lyric, Penthouse's Hot Talk, Trouser Press Record Guide* and *The Village Voice.*

• ?/?/88 Tom Krontenmacher, who presents himself as a reporter covering the Brom story for *Rolling Stone,* sees the *Twin Cities Reader* article and calls Negativland seeking an interview. Negativland declines to comment.

• 5/11/88 After seeing the *BAM* article, a news producer for CBS Television's San Francisco affiliate, KPIX Channel 5, calls Negativland to request a televised interview. Negativland does not decline this opportunity to reach millions with its message. TV reporter Hal Eisner arrives in the KPIX mobile Electronic News Gathering unit. During the interview Negativland maintains the rumored link to the Brom case, but continue to state that they are unable to discuss details of the case. Much of the interview time is spent discussing the American news media, their appetite for the sensational, their tendency to create their own "news," and related topics. All of this discussion is cut from the aired tape. Like the other reports to date, Channel 5 takes the purported connection for granted, but this time in a sensationalized feature piece emphasizing links between music and murder including footage of the Brom family being carried from their home in body bags.

• 5/14/88 After seeing the Channel 5 news lead story, the *San Francisco Chronicle* religion writer calls Negativland requesting an interview. The group again claims they're unable to discuss the case, but do describe various real and imagined effects that the onslaught of publicity has had on the group. The *Chronicle* prints an article restating the proposed connection, but gets many of the "facts" wrong, as a result of their dependence on other media stories as their only source material. It's now abundantly clear that the major source for news is other news.

• 6/3/88 David Brom is transferred to the Oakes Treatment Center for severely emotionally disturbed children and adolescents in Austin, Texas.

• 6/7/88 The *Village Voice* publishes an article on the Negativland-Brom link. Media critic R.J. Smith recounts the original press release's version of the rumored connection with some skepticism. In researching this piece, Smith and *Voice* media critic Jeffrey Stokes go so far as to track down a Negativland member at his job for confirmation of the story. The group, by now apprehensive that their monstrous joke may have become completely uncontrollable, refuses to answer questions on the phone, citing previous reporters' editing and distortion of their comments. Negativland does, however, agree to send a prepared written statement. Smith also reports con-

tacting San Francisco FBI spokesman Chuck Latting, who says of Negativland, "To the best of my knowledge, we've had no contact with them."
• 6/19/88 The *San Francisco Chronicle's* pop music critic, Joel Selvin, devotes two-thirds of his weekly column to the Negativland-Brom story. The group also declines to be interviewed in this article, and Selvin is sent a copy of the same statement the *Voice* received, which he accurately reproduced. "As to our uncertain association with the Brom case, we think it's foolish and will comment no further. For a while, we made comments to the press and found that we were so misquoted and events so misstated to fit the writer's need to grab attention and the editor's need to abbreviate that we will now make no more statements whatsoever. Sensationalism reigns."
• 8/1/88 Negativland decides to make a somewhat musical depiction of this entire media odyssey. It began as a 12-inch single, but quickly expands to a full LP side.
• 12/9/88 Minnesota Supreme Court rules that Brom be tried as an adult. Arraignment is set for January, 1989. David Brom awaits trial.

The Last Word
Somewhere beneath the media representation of the Brom murders is an inexplicable human tragedy. Our act of creating a false association with such a tragedy is open to ethical interpretation.

We all swim in an ocean of mass media that fills our minds with people and events with which we have no actual contact at all. We commonly absorb these media presences as part of our own "reality," even though any media experience consists only of one-way, edited representations of reality. Negativland uses this electronic environment of factual fictions as both source and subject for much of our work, keeping in mind that to experience a picture of a thing is not to experience the thing.

Our lie was intended for and directed to the *media,* and it proved very effective in exposing the unreliable process of cannibalization that passes for "news." Negativland chose to exploit the media's appetite for particularly sensational stories by becoming a subject they couldn't resist—the latest version of a ridiculous media cliche that proposes that rock song lyrics instigate murder. Common sense suggests that murderers purchase records that appeal to them, just as they purchase the weapons they use.

Helter Stupid is about the media menu of illusions we all eat from, as well as an attempt to materialize our perception of Negativland as a bogus subject for the voracious media meat grinder.

Like all good hoaxes, this one got out of hand. Negativland loosed a type of media virus that—given the autophagous appetite and sensationalist, tabloid mentality of the newsmedia—spread like anthrax.

It can be said of Negativland that they invented their own genre and that no other sound outfit has taken found footage and chance encounters as far. Yet neither of these factoids determined the nature and the extent of this festival of rumor reported as fact. It was sufficient for the group to have created a suitably controversial work, "Christianity is Stupid," and for the Imp of the Perverse to inspire them to put out the initial bit of disinformation. *After the print and broadcast newsmedia were infected, it remained only for the group to stay mum on the matter. Yet early in 1990, long after the story was exposed as false, sparks still flew. The group fretted about reprisals from a local TV station for the unauthorized use of sound snippets and from David Brom's lawyer, who sought compensation for their use of his client's image in the cover graphic for their new release,* Helter Stupid.

I came to the following interview as no stranger to the altered state known as Negativland. I'd guested on "Over the Edge," a weekly radio program with group members, since the early '80s when I first saw them in performance. In an era of unusual acts, there's stood out. Weatherman David Willis lectures on cleanliness while scrubbing the monitors with 409, the action spills offstage to a table where a toaster rigged never to pop cinders a slice of Wonderbread. First the appalling aroma of toasting bread, then the somewhat alarming burning smell as black smoke poured out. That attraction/ repulsion factor seemed to run throughout the group's output of live shows, records and radio programming. It made it all the more apropos when they were allowed to mix live during the KPFA-FM broadcast of Reagan's second inaugural address. Soon the fast and dense information of their albums began to get more and more attention as did their phantom live shows wherein they stayed in their studio while the mix was pumped out to far away venues through a hyper-clear phone line. Negativland issued international passports.

A willingness to criticize as well as praise the brain children of Negativland made the discussion all the more lively. At one point I asked R.U. Sirius, "Can this be an argument?" I wanted to provoke Don and Mark to go beyond the replies they'd already made to the charge that they were guilty of a grotesque exploitation of a hideous event. Their most sustained concept piece, Helter Stupid, *a painstaking examination and explicit commentary on the ensuing media vortex that resulted from a hardly credible press release, demanded more than a facile discussion. They had ridden out the first wave of allegations and accusations and had just released this rather obsessive remix of the public events and behind-the-scenes skullduggery. They were now in a position to step out from behind their wall of sound and exhibit some of their more guarded feelings.*

Andre Breton said, "Beauty must be convulsive or not at all." My own saying is "An artist will be obsessive or not at all." Both of these statements apply to Helter Stupid, *Negativland's most compelling work.*

It was a wintry night in Northern California as we pulled into MONDO 2000's *technogothic citadel in the hills...*

Stephan Ronan

MONDO 2000: *Helter Stupid* **is a very different entity from the** *Dick Vaughn Memorial Music Saga* **that's on side two. The name of the album is** *Helter Stupid* **but** *Helter Stupid* **is really definitely one side and not the other.**
DJ: There is so much to be gleaned from "The Perfect Cut" (Side 2 of *Helter Stupid*). All that radio production stuff and everything is so sleazy and cynical.
MH: Well, Don, do you think that we're gonna be wallowing in cynicism and irony for the rest of our careers or are we gonna actually start coming out and having some

opinions on things and not always being completely glib. Actually I don't think *Helter Stupid*'s completely ironic.

M2: *Helter Stupid*'s kind of like a documentary.

DJ: Yeah. It's a pseudo-totally-bashed-up documentary.

MH: I think we're generally very careful to leave things open. To let the listener draw his own conclusions.

Like "Time Zones" on *Escape From Noise*. It's just two guys talking about how many time zones there are in the Soviet Union. That's all it is. But as you listen to it, it becomes much more than that. They're talking about us vs. them, about power, about fear and the size of their country vs. the size of ours.

M2: That's why I referred to *Helter Stupid* as a documentary, and like all documentaries it's not really objective. You're led to draw the conclusion that news is cannibalistic. That news is not so much interested in reportage and the truth as in not being scooped. And they're grabbing their news from somebody else and recombining it... sensationalism, all those things are really rather explicit in that piece. You can't not think those things after...

MH: Right! With *Helter Stupid* we're actually coming forward and... I don't know how to put it exactly...

DJ: Coming forward, we're moving backward, that's how I'd put it.

MH: Well, in many ways there's far less ambiguity.

M2: OK, but *Helter Stupid* is not just the audio *Helter Stupid*. It's also the chronology and it's the essay on the events. Therefore it's quite a package. And it's quite a convincing package. And I take no issue with the conclusion other than to say it's not subtle. It's no longer inflective. You guys are not being elusive or obfuscating or just sort of implying what your critique, or your irony, might be. You're pretty much spelling it out.

DJ: Here's the reason for that. We went through this whole experience and then we decided to make a record. It came out as this total jumbled-up mess of found stuff. In this case it had a kind of pseudo-documentary feel to it. But still, if you listened to the record, you will learn practically nothing about the actual event that the record was stimulated by. It doesn't tell the story. It uses a few people who were involved in the actual event, in terms of found audio stuff, but it doesn't tell the story. You wouldn't even know what the whole issue is if you had nothing but that record to listen to.

M2: Without the documentation that comes with it.

DJ: The newscast gives you the most information of anything on the record. So in looking at that we said, "You know, this really doesn't explain enough. And it needs to be explained, because we're going to get accused of exploiting a tragic murder."

MH: I'm realizing that there's no way that we can get out of the fact that we have. We didn't mean to, but we have and we might as well cop to it.

DJ: That's the reason that we put all of that very specific documentation inside. To both explain the event and explain our position in pursuing it. Which is to somehow get inside how the media works, particularly the news media, and bring that out as a subject, and as a source for our work. I don't think people would get that without documentation.

MH: In all Negativland records, the packaging has always been an important part of the presentation.

M2: Mark was saying that it was a good thing that you made this statement about exploiting a tragic event in that it's at least clear that you view it as a tragic event. My immediate reaction was "Oh! The Royal Disclaimer!" Which is just like all the way through the process you guys maintained the disclaimer, "We never said this was true. We said we didn't know about it." I thought we suddenly had a breakthrough when you said "we have exploited"... but you were saying we have been *accused* of exploiting it. You're still sort of evading the point. Didn't Negativland exploit...

MH: Yes. Of course we did. I realize that we did.

DJ: Of course we did. But I hope this is not the point that people take away from the record. Because if we thought that was the main message, I don't think we would have recorded it. Everyone in the group was very uncomfortable about that aspect of it all the way through. Now that aspect exists. We are selling records that are based on a murder—using this subject to sell our next record. But there's other important points that can only be made by exploiting this particular subject that the news media *could not resist* dealing with. They didn't resist, so they took it down their path of cannibalization to an ultimate end. And that's what we saw happening and that's what we wanted to pursue. Not the fact of this actual murder.

M2: No. In fact the audio track of *Helter Stupid* doesn't exploit the murder. It exploits the media coverage of the alleged link between your song, "Christianity Is Stupid," and the murder.

DJ: And then it goes deeper into being about the media and violence. It's kind of a series of abstract ruminations and meditations.

M2: There is only one point at which you exploit the murder and that's the press release. And, in fact, SST Records could have let it die. And any number of the media people could have let it die... ignored it. It's obvious from the packaging that it was rather farfetched and it was ridiculously gullible for anyone to accept it without substantial fact checking.

DJ: You'd think so, but the fact is that very few facts are checked.

M2: *Time* magazine has narrowed down its fact checkers to a staff of three. It used to be a staff of 100.

DJ: If they read it, they believe it. That's how it works now.

M2: When the news media reads *other* news media, they believe it. I'm probably a few steps more irresponsible than you in that I don't really give a shit if you exploit a person's murder of his parent.

DJ: You would if they were sitting here!

M2: Perhaps. But in an objective sense I don't, because media exploits them every day.

MH: That's part of our point. And what we're trying to address, too, is that these murders really happened. This is horrible. If you try to actually imagine what he did. He took an ax. He chopped up four other people. And it's like when you think about it...

DJ:... in the middle of the night. While you're sleeping...

MH: It's beyond anything you and I can really comprehend.

M2: I'm for total liberty over moral restraint, but this isn't an interview about me.

DJ: In a way, every artist is above moral restrain in that they'll use everything as grist for the mill. We do. But the point is that you want in some way to distance yourself from the actual reality. You have to in order to do that. And that's what we tried to do with the total packaging of this. I don't want to meet the relatives of those people. I don't want to talk to friends of the family. It'd be very embarrassing. But I think the artist has to distance himself from that in order to produce anything that's of any critical importance or value. 'Cause it always involves somebody else's feelings.

M2: I've given you this license and, in fact, I'm finding a level of defensiveness in you guys that I would just as soon dispense with, because you don't have to defend it, at least to this interviewer.

MH: The reason I was making the point about the actual grisly reality of it is because this is something that *really* happened in the world. What we were dealing with was a story, a fiction, the news... factual fictions as Don has called it... about an ax murder. We weren't dealing with what really happened. What has happened since is that, in fact, the news did get back to the boy. That I find really disturbing. The news got back to the lawyers and the family and the newspapers. And we've been called by papers in Rochester, Minnesota, and we've been called by papers in Minneapolis. Now the record's come out. And to me, it's getting to be too *weird*. I don't want to think about that reality. We've tangled ourselves up in this thing now, and for the people in that town who knew the family and the boy, it's not just a story. It really happened. They know this kid, or they know his friends and his family. It's becoming increasingly disturbing and complex, when the intent of the record was to kind of settle it. The idea was that the record would be our statement and then we could say, "OK, leave us alone. Listen to the record and that'll explain what was going on."

M2: It's a case of the medium being the message. It's the fact that you put out a record based on this whole incident—and not what's actually on the record— that becomes news. So you're just further involving yourselves.

MH: I talked to one news guy. He kept asking me questions and I kept saying, "Look, I don't really want to talk to you. You have an agenda. You're reporting on this for your town. You're gonna take anything I say and make it fit whatever your agenda is." And I said, "Really, all your questions can be answered by listening to the record. Listen to the record, read the liner notes. Listen to the record again, read the liner notes again, and hopefully you will understand what we're trying to say."

M2: They want you to give them that little sound byte of culpability so they can frame you as these heartless guys that exploited murder. But what I'm saying is that the news, as infotainment, is totally devoid of *true* human sympathies and feelings. They use the sham of sympathy to increase the salability of a product that they're selling. They have no moral high ground to stand on from which to judge you guys. And in fact they are the worst exploiters of every tragic crime

and...

DJ: They have a lot higher ground than we do. They have a TV tower and we don't!

M2: That's higher profile. That's not higher moral ground. Noam Chomsky called his book *The Manufacture of Consent*. So what the news media does is manufacture moral indignation. That's the point that I want to move to with this. What you guys did by this hoax is that you've completely drawn out everything back to "Helter Skelter," and the aligning of the Beatles' song to those mass murders, right up to the current Tipper Gore Mothers-Against-Dirty-Satanic-Rock-Songs situation. So what you've done, using the resonance of all this stuff, is show how they're champing at the bit to present it as fact. And to make all these linkages that amount to shit..

DJ: You got it. It's a monstrous joke!

M2: Has anyone looked further into the murder? Was there any argument about music between this kid and his parents? They report it as if that's a fact.

MH: I'll tell you a bizarre coincidence, or synchronicity as we say in California. As it turned out, someone who is in a band that's on the same label that we're on knew the family when he was younger. And it turns out that the boy had posters of other SST bands on his wall. This kid was into, you know, punk... hardcore. So recently we found out that SST actually had David Brom on their mailing list. He used to order records from mail order.

M2: So he had heard you guys.

MH: No, I don't think he ever did.

M2: He at least saw your name.

MH: I don't know. At this point he knows who we are. We've heard that his lawyer got a hold of the record and now they're threatening to take us to court. So David Brom knows about us. Now I'm feeling even more weird. What have we done? Imagine this one human being who did that, who has to live with that the rest of his life, and who has a record album that has his picture on the cover. It's really disturbing.

M2: I wouldn't be totally shocked to learn that David Brom gets fans of his own...

DJ: And he's writing a book...

M2: What discontented precocious teenager hasn't thought about dispatching his family?

MH: I never did!

M2: You never did? You loved your mom and pop?

MH: Well enough not to think of killing them. I enjoyed watching other people kill their parents but I never considered doing it.

M2: I'm interested in the fact that this was entered into semi-accidentally. You didn't know it was going to come to this level of intensity. And you kind of followed the course of the disease, and now everybody is pretty well poisoned.

MH: When you go back to the original mutant, there's a shadowy figure in Negativland that doesn't turn up at their interviews and this incident totally fits him.

DJ: (Laughing) He appears on the back cover.

M2: Yeah, Richard. To me this whole thing somehow organically connects to

him, and grows out of him, although the others have watered the plant and tended the garden.

DJ: He's the member where the name Negativland *really* applies. He's the archetypal negative sort of imp. It was he who started the whole thing in a sort of offhand way.

MH: It was just that we had to cancel a tour because the tour was going to lose money and we can't afford to lose money because we don't make a lot. So we decided to cancel it in a more interesting way. And we'd already been getting some indications—from some other press releases—that the news media was not very careful in how it presented information. So we just did it as a sort of experiment. Richard came up with this press release.

He wrote it up and presented it to us, and we said, "That's kind of an interesting idea, Richard. Gee, well, let's see what happens." It wasn't like "This is a good publicity stunt." It was more like let's let this little virus out and see what happens." Most of the group thought it would go nowhere because—as you were pointing out earlier—it seemed to be very easy to check out and find that it wasn't true.

M2: Before sending it out, did you stop at any moment and imagine that it might turn out as peculiarly as it...

MH: ...never! Never in a million years! And we certainly never thought that it would turn into our next album.

It's such a strange thing to see. This person is reprinting this story and then this person's reprinting *his* story and it's growing and yet no one's checking to see if it's true. And it's just another story. But see how it developed. You're rolling from a lie to a very legitimate looking thing.

M2: There also had to be a decision on the part of you guys that you weren't going to try to stop it, refute it, and tell the first interviewer that called you that...

MH; But you have to realize that this was happening in front of us and we were just playing along as it happened wondering "What do we do now?" We kept having meetings and eventually we decided that we weren't going to say anything more. That's it. We're done talking to the media. We will not stimulate the media in any way by making any comments because we want to leave this experiment as pure as we can. However, when Channel 5 TV News called up... well, "I'm not passing *this* up. This is too bizarre." And they wanted to interview us in our own home. So we sort of reluctantly agreed to let them do it.

I also saw a TV appearance as an opportunity to try to talk about some of the issues involved in how the media works. At the time, we weren't ready to admit this was a hoax. But it seemed like a great opportunity to deal with electronic news. So we did during that interview. For two hours cameras rolled and we talked all about how the news is edited reality and how it's all sound bytes and sensationalized, and it's entertainment and, of course, they didn't use any of that at all.

They were promising us they weren't going to sensationalize this and they were going to try to address the issues that it raised. I could tell the guy was just bullshitting me because he wanted to get his story.

M2: The headline of the press release was "Negativland Tour Axed at Last Minute." Similarly, Alfred Hitchcock said, "People think that I'm a monster" because he

was a black humorist. **The majority of people think they like black humor if they get it in little diluted doses....**

MH: I'll tell you something funny that happened that we didn't mention in the chronology. A month after we put out the first press release, we put out *another* press release saying there was an uproar going on because people were writing to Ann Landers saying Negativland's song "Nesbitt's Lime Soda" was giving bees a bad rap for stinging people on the tongue. The release also said that the Beekeeper Association of America was complaining about our song. We sent this out as a press release thinking, "This will stop it. They'll get the idea that this is a joke.

DJ: This is a series of joke press releases.

MH: And the bee release, of course, went nowhere because that wasn't of interest.

At a certain point, SST decided they no longer wanted to put out any more information associating themselves with this thing. They were concerned for themselves legally. We told the label to refer all phone calls to the band. We weren't asking them to cover for us. We didn't want to compromise their integrity in any way.

M2: A lot of black humor is like acts of spontaneous inappropriate behavior that most people control... where you get this really weird twisted idea and it seems so great that you just have to do it. It's pure id.

DJ: I always like to do those things.

MH: That's part of how we work in the studio. We don't sit down and really write a composition. We have some ideas to start with and we're messing around and accidents happen. You stumble across something, some sound event and you say, "This is much better than our idea." And the way we worked on this press release is really similar to how we worked on our live shows or our records or anything else. We just sort of follow this thing where it seems to want to go.

M2: Stephen was referring to *Helter Stupid* as sort of being a documentary. My response to listening to the record was that it was much more intense, in an emotional sense, than anything else I've heard from Negativland. I don't know if that's something that I brought with me knowing the story behind the record. It's almost like a very intense jazz piece. It's got a lot of drive.

DJ: That's partly because it's so long and unbroken and continuous. I think we've done little things that are just as intense. I wanted to keep the same thing up all the way through. I wanted the overkill, which is like my impression of the media.

I think the structure is about information overload, although personally I don't ever find myself overloaded with information and I can listen to three things at the same time and actually comprehend what's going on.

M2: But what makes this piece so arresting is not merely that it's overload, because it's always overload with Negativland. That's the palette you're going to be working with, an overloaded palette. What you're going to paint is going to be different every time. And it begins with this incredibly gripping sound, so right away you're tense, you feel like you're under attack.

DJ: Did you play it backwards? (General laughter)

M2. That first gripping sound?

MH: For our readers at home: take the beginning of side one of *Helter Stupid* and play it backwards.

M2: While I think of it, let me ask you this. Part of this whole Tipper Gore rock-and-satanism epoch is the backward masking controversy. This is very much an element of your piece.

DJ: Wait. Wait. Before you go on—you assumed that our palette was overloaded and it was always going to be overloaded. That's not true and, in fact, our next record might be completely different and very relaxed.

M2: Negativland in the Heart of Space.

DJ: Yeah, that's it. We do that kind of stuff.

M2: It'll be your *John Wesley Harding*...

DJ: I hope it's as interesting.

M2: On "Stupid" the theme of backward masking comes up. Do you guys have any info on this? Is there even the slightest evidence that there's any reality to it?

MH: It's completely silly, right?

DJ: How could you understand something if it's backwards? The people who are into this say that it *does* penetrate your brain in the same sense that sleep tapes do.

M2: Well, that's the contention, but I don't see any proof.

DJ: No, there isn't any proof. There's no proof that it works.

MH: I think you could argue that if, at a barely audible level you inserted someone saying, "Kill your parents, kill your parents"...

M2: That's forward, though.

MH: I could see how that... I wouldn't exactly support someone doing that.

M2: That's how subliminal suggestion is supposed to work but...

MH: Don did a whole radio show relating to *Helter Stupid* and backward masking. As I was listening to it I was thinking, you know, this is so silly. How could they even discuss this and not be embarrassed for themselves. The idea that anyone could even think for a second that you could understand that...

M2: These are the people who believe that the beast will come and everyone will have to do business with the mark of 666. So it's a very small leap for them to believe that backward masking is intelligible to the brain.

MH: ...hpargarap a ekil tsuj ,sdrawkcab ti evah tsuj dna weivretni eht fo trap emos esu uoy fI ?od dluohs uoy tahw wonk uoy, etunim a tiaW

DJ: I'm not sure whether the original idea of what is supposed to be potent about backward masking is that you would be playing these records forwards and you would pass this section that if you heard it backwards would be saying something different from what it is saying forwards—or whether the idea was that every record you buy, you're supposed to go home and play the whole thing backwards just to see if anything's there—and then when you hear it, it will...

M2: You know, all of this goes back to that great enemy of Christianity, John Lennon. Because it was John Lennon who began to use the sound of backward guitars, backward vocals. "Rain" was the first pop song to use that. In fact, it goes another step backward to William Burroughs, Brian Gyson, and Ian

113

Somerville's experiments in London where Paul McCartney had rented a studio for them. They were doing all these kinds of things and that's how The Beatles came to be interested. Of course, it was for sound experimentation, not for subliminal suggestion or brainwashing or anything like that.

MH: Yeah. The first time I remember turning a tape backwards on a reel-to-reel it was really wonderful. Wow, listen to this! It sounds great."

M2: Once you have that as another groovy guitar sound, it's going to be imitated. And then, decades later you have someone contending that backward masking is a way to do mind-fucking things with your music. Then, of course, people like Ozzie or whoever are going to start actually using backward masking. And naturally, on occasion, they'll say "Hail Satan!" So when the Christians decide the point of backward masking is to indoctrinate people to Satanism, you're going to have people who are going to exploit that, aren't you?

DJ: Hmmm, Hail Satan... good idea, you know? Why didn't I think of that?

MH: There's always an argument about whether the media causes people to commit crimes. Do songs cause people to worship satan or kill their parents? And I think it's absolutely clear that kids who are growing up on a diet of *Dirty Harry* and *Friday The 13th*—they have a whole weird inner vocabulary related to how to react and respond in emotional situations and crisis situations. And in violent situations. I've been threatened at gunpoint by kids whose body language tells me they've picked it up from TV Shows.

M2: The whole social ritual of heterosexual romance is learned from the movies.

MH: So the whole argument is ridiculous because it's obvious that, in this century, the media is part of the sea we're swimming in. Obviously, it has everything to do with how you end up behaving.

DJ: It's definitely dangerous that people are confusing reality with fiction. But you see that mostly in really young kids. I don't think it's really that effective with older people. To some extent, we're overly fearful about how much we can take in and deal with.

M2: It's more of a direct factor in political behavior than in personal. It's like some of us can synthesize the information and have it make sense. But that breakdown between what's real and what's not winds up being bizarre things like universal support for the invasion of Panama. And on the level of international news, it's all getting closer and more intense and more immediate and at the same time more unreal. And I think that has to do both with the overload and the increasingly flimsy way in which the news media contextualizes stuff.

DJ: That's a good point. The media covers everything from intensely personal fictions to the vast view of the world. And what's pretending to be the news is almost as fictitious. Most people's view of the big world out there comes purely through television. But they have a lot of other reference points for their personal lives. They can look around and say, "Gee, I'm not like Oprah Winfrey, you know? I'm really not." But they look at Panama, and they really don't know whether that's true or not, because they have no personal reference points. So they more or less accept whatever they're told.

M2: We can't even talk about the political aspects. I'm trying to get to the psychological aspects, my point being Hinkley could not have been induced to shoot Reagan merely by seeing *Taxi Driver* had his better judgment not already been destroyed through psychosis.

DJ: That's my point in the "Helter Stupid" editorial, you have to already be the killer before you start buying this killer music.

M2: Then you look for a soundtrack. You look for the accompaniment that appeals to you.

Going Over the Edge on LSD or Media

MH: I find that I'm able to follow certain things better if I'm a little bit over-engaged, if my brain is just a little bit over-engaged with a little bit too much input. I'm able to read the book better if I've got the record on and I'm eating.

DJ: It's just the modern way to get educated.

M2: Being able to enjoy your radio show "Over the Edge (Don Joyce hosts a radio show on KPFA 94.1 FM, Berkeley, Thursday nights at midnight) is an acquired thing. Like the first time most people hear it, they find there's too much going on. It's too busy. It's too distracting, it's too incoherent. It's too much of a cacophony. Then, after a while, they begin to sort of get in the swim of it, like it, even want to participate and add themselves to it.

DJ: A lot of people have their first positive responses by realizing it's sort of like a dream.

M2: The dream is, of course, the one altered state of consciousness that this culture can't dispense with yet. So it's like LSD. People's first impressions are often, "It's too much. I can't handle it." You know—uh-oh! And then they get to a state where they're a little bit spellbound, still apprehensive, not completely grooving with it. And then, if they're lucky and they're not going to have a terrible fearful duration of the trip, they might even get to enjoy the sensory overload, because that's essentially what LSD does— inhibit the sensory inhibitors so that you get a sensory overload. Being able to enjoy "Over the Edge" or Negativland or acid is sort of the same thing because it's about being able to process all the input you're getting and have it be coherent. Which creates a kind of *physical* pleasure.

MH: It's interesting to me how different people of different ages and occupations react to what we do, the music we do, because, you know, I've talked to some people who are in the computer hacker class of brain and they listen to Negativland and find it sort of pleasantly engaging—because it's got enough information in it. Rudy Rucker, in your last issue, was defining cyberpunk as something with a high density of information. So to kids who are growing up with video games and computers in their home and all that, it probably just seems like easy listening.

M2: It's odd that you're using television as your reference point for what you're doing in radio and sound.

DJ: Television is an indicator of a certain age of when everything became electronic.

MH: And you could change the channels.

DJ: Change the channels!

M2:: As art theory evolved in the '80s, the hallmark of post-modernism has turned out to be appropriation. And it goes back a long way. Somehow it seemed more important to use recombined images that were supplied you through the media—through whatever source you got them from—then manufacturing or drawing something wholly new. And in audio, this is what Negativland came along and was doing. And not just Negativland, but Cabaret Voltaire and Throbbing Gristle—using a lot of found stuff and recontextualizing it.

MH: They all stopped doing it after a pretty short amount of time. It went from a foreground to a background element in a lot of that work.

M2: : And then there's the pop diffusion of it, Big Audio Dynamite and a lot of the rap groups...

MH: Well, it's become *de rigeur*. And it makes me wonder about what we're doing, because when we started it was an area that needed exploring. Now, ten years later, we've done a lot of that spelunking and it's now reached the point that found sounds, sampled bits of noise taped off the media, are an excepted part of the pop vocabulary.

M2: It's always been legally controversial, and that aspect is reaching a crescendo now with your album and John Oswald's *Plunderphonics* and the de la Soul lawsuit...

MH: Right. But let me finish my point. It's no longer clear to me if we're really on the edge any more with what we're doing. It seems to me now like we're inside the fence, you know?

M2: I would put you on the edge simply because of your high visibility and influence. I mean, edge people are always working in obscurity. Or from another point of view, you can't see the edge any more.

MH: It's really hard to see any totally new direction. It's all appropriation.

M2: When you started back in '78—'79, did you right away begin supplying new contexts for found materials?

MH: Yes, even before I was recording—just fooling around—I used to mix recordings of game shows and TV bits and sounds I'd recorded on the street and glass breaking and tape loops and the radio was always on with some distorted AM channel...

DJ: We've been more and more willing to accept the actual content of the found stuff and let it stand on its own power.

M2: That's the progression I want to address...

MH: From the beginning, it was just what we wanted to hear. When Negativland started, I was buying a lot of independent music, and was starting to find out that there was this whole other world out there. I liked a lot of what I heard, but there was definitely something missing that I wanted to hear. So I started mixing in all this stuff from my world, you know, my dog barking, the sprinklers on outside, and the TV was always on. It was a totally naive thing really. And the more I started working with that, the more I started thinking about the content. So I started carrying around notebooks and writing my observations down. I'd go though all the commercials I'd record from radio stations, and I'd write down all my favorites lines and edit them out and filled up libraries, and Don, of course, had done that on a massive scale for years. He had a huge library of edited-down bits.

M2: You weren't aware that psychedelic groups had done that first, including The Beatles?

MH: No I wasn't.

M2: So from 1978– 1979, these sounds were an element of your music, but you also provided a lot of the vocals and instrumental elements and stuff. But now, in 1990, we have a record with no vocals by you guys.

DJ: Right, it's basically all made up of media.

M2: Which is not the case with *Escape from Noise*.

DJ: It's like we sort of disappeared in a way. The media, it's all just the media speaking for us now.

MH: There aren't even credits on *Helter Stupid*. We didn't even say who made it anymore. Our own idiosyncratic personalities are much more in evidence on *Escape from Noise*—the songs, the lyrics, the little stories. And those are now gone.

M2: That's what I was wondering. I saw this record as an anomaly for that reason and I'm thinking that you guys have committed a bit of rock 'n' roll suicide—I suspect deliberately. You've done something other than a commercial shot. Because what is missing from this is hits—potential singles that can be pulled for college radio—like "Car Bomb" and others on the last one.

DJ: But *Escape from Noise* wasn't conceived to have any hooky hits either. It did really well on college radio, but even "Christianity Is Stupid" doesn't have "hooks." There were never any intentions about that, one way or another.

M2: I see *Helter Stupid* as Volume 2 of *Escape From Noise*.

MH: As a matter of fact, if you look at the packaging of *Escape From Noise* and *Helter Stupid* you will see that they look the same. It's got a color photo in the center with text around it, and a heading across... We decided to make the design visually contiguous.

M2: I see "The Perfect Cut" as the search for a B side.

MH: Well the title is a bit of black humor since all of side A is in reference to an ax murder.

I think we're going to get pigeonholed as a media manipulation band. We've always manipulated media sounds, but now we're actually manipulating in the sense of neo-yippie pranks.

DJ: First, with *Escape From Noise* doing well—that broke us away from our earlier suburban noise band image, I think. Now with *Helter Stupid* we're really gonna get pegged.

M2: You always had a sound, but your sound has really solidified into *your* sound. It's not a bad thing.

MH: But this record's sound is actually based on mid-'70s disco records and it has really bizarre production values. It's not modern sounding at all. It's not even *our* sound. It's all stolen.

M2: The B side is obviously a '70s revival parody.

DJ: That's one of the reasons did it.

MH: Actually, that's a nice sort of subtext. "The Perfect Cut" is a comment on nostalgia as a commodity. OK, now we're going to sell you the '70s, a really crappy, ugly, tacky decade. We can even sell *that* to you.

THREE BODIES OF WORK

M2: I'd like the voices of Negativland members to come back.

MH: Don't worry, they will. I've been working on writing song lyrics and singing for the last couple of years, but none of that work ended up fitting into what we're doing. There's a body of work that hasn't really jelled yet. There's a body of unfinished work now that...

DJ: There's about three bodies...

MH: ...that are so different from anything we've done. And it's gonna be fun to put those out and confuse our fans.

I DON'T WANNA TALK TO THE LAWYERS

MH: I think we're all gonna get in more trouble over *Helter Stupid* that I ever imagined. I mean, I sure never imagined we'd hear from David Brom's lawyers.

M2: Well are you litigable in that connection.

MH: I don't know.

M2: Can we get into the legal ramifications of appropriation?

MH: Well, I'm really ignorant about art history. So I just recently read a book by Calvin Tompkins called *Off The Wall* about John Cage, Rauschenberg and Merce Cunningham and all that. And it was fun finding these kindred spirits or kindred brain functions. It was fun to see that that stuff was going on many many years ago.

DJ: There were always legal questions, going back to Andy Warhol with his exact same-sized copies of Brillo boxes and so forth, but it came to nothing.

MH: It's become rampant now 'cause of technology.

M2: At first, Warhol was copying logos, painting replicas. But then when he started taking news photos and silk screening them into multiples and so forth, that's really a level of appropriation very analogous to what you guys do... using the actual thing. You don't do a parody of the news guy, you *use* the news guy.

MH: That was important to *Helter Stupid*. We decided we'd do this chronology and not make generalizations about the media. We decided we were gonna be really specific. We're gonna let the writer who was idiotic say his name. We're gonna use the name of the TV station. And that's getting us in trouble too.

It's very clear that the record is a criticism of the media. And I'm very interested in engaging with anyone who we're criticizing directly in the work. I want direct conversation. I don't wanna talk to the lawyers. I wanna be face to face with that guy and say, "Look, what do you really think about what we did? Because we're trying to make a real point."

DJ: I kind of like the idea of the news suing an artist.

Is culture something that can be used without permission, or isn't it? I think it should be. You should be able to use anything that's in the literal public domain.

MH: But you could ask where one draws that line.

M2: I've got the perfect hypothetical situation. What if a minute or more of one of your things showed up in someone else's record.

MH: It's been done!

DJ: And that was fine.

118

MH: The number of people who've heard about our connection with this story greatly outnumbers the number of people that will hear the record. The number of people that hear the record are going to outnumber the people who actually buy the record. The number of people who buy it will outnumber those who really listen to it and read the liner notes. The number of people who read the liner notes and really get what we're saying and think about it will be outnumbered by those who don't. So—in fact—what's going to happen is we're going to end up perpetuating this hoax and this myth about ourselves to a large number of people.

I mean twenty years from now, I'm going to run into someone who's going to say, "Oh, yeah. You killed that kid in Minnesota."

Civilizing the Electronic Frontier

The foundation of the Electronic Frontier Foundation was undoubtedly a seminal event in the history of cyberspace. I recall going to the initiatory meeting somewhere in the South Bay. It was at the imposingly beautiful home of a wealthy computer software programmer (I forget who) and the streets outside were lined with MGs, BMWs, and other autos of affluence. If not for the trappings of wealth, it might have been an SDS meeting in 1969. Here was a crowd of hairy, irreverent, anti-government types united by the need to deal with the oppressive actions of the police establishment. It made me optimistic about the future. Later I would come to view this crowd, with some degree of suspicion, as a self-interest group. And while the activities of the EFF are mostly valid, they did not represent the renewal of revolutionary vigor that I had hoped for. Having said that, I should also say that John Perry Barlow gets an awful lot of shit lately. I guess people are tired of his rap, but I think this interview ought to provide a reminder that the old libertarian cyberspace cowboy produces some downright insightful bullshit some of the time. Mitch Kapor ain't no slouch either.

An Interview with Mitch Karop & John Barlow of the
Electronic Frontier Foundation
R.U. Sirius with David Gans

Space may be the final frontier, but there's at least one more earthbound arena for the social-political struggle before it's time to start worrying about Martian mineral rights and the exploitation of Betelgeusian guest workers. Electronics.

The United States Constitution and the Bill of Rights were created in the era of hand-set type, before the telegraph, telephone or broadcast media. Each new wave of technology has pushed at the boundaries of liberty and tugged at the coattails of authority by enabling more rapid and comprehensive dissemination of information. There's more communication taking place outside the purview of centalized authority as well as more light shed on the workings of government and business. For a long time now, drugs have been seen by the government as the main threat to its control of knowledge and information. Since the 1960s, the particular species of vegetable that I sometimes carry in my pocket could, if found by the wrong person, land me in jail and lose me my property.

Now it's my disk drive.

The advent of personal computers and modems, coupled with the immense penetration of the telephone network, threatens the hegemony of the government/corporate paradigm by empowering millions of individuals. In the 90s, thanks to desktop communication, it is not longer necessary to "publish" "revolutionary" documents in the old sense of the word. Information can be propagated across thousands of miles in all directions in a matter of moments and it can't be stopped short of dismantling the entire telephone system. This genie can never be put back in the bottle. But that hasn't discouraged the Enforcement Community from doing its saurian best to try.

Acting on requests from certain corporations, the FBI and the Secret Service—

armed with vaguely worded warrants—have raided businesses and the homes of private citizens and seized tremendous numbers of computers and related items with very few corresponding arrests. The language on the warrants was vague because even in the rare case when the government knows what it's looking for, on the electronic frontier, it probably has no idea what it's looking at.

So here I am watching a beautiful July sunset from the deck of a home overlooking Silicon Valley, participating in a good-natured but urgent gathering sponsored by the two founders of the Electronic Frontier Foundation, Mitch Kapor and John Barlow. Their alliance began with an arguably pointless act: someone, probably an employee of Apple computer, "liberated" a relatively minor piece of Macintosh operating code and sent it, over the signature of "NuPrometheus League," to a number of industry figures. Mitch Kapor, founder of Lotus Development Corporation, was one of the lucky recipients. Kapor immediately inferred that the mysterious floppy was nothing more politically significant than an attempt to infect his computer with a virus, and sent it back.

John Barlow, Grateful Dead lyricist and writer about things cyber, didn't receive a floppy disk from NuPrometheus, but because he attended the fifth hackers conference in October 1989, he *did* received a visit from an FBI agent regarding NuPrometheus. Investigating Agent Baxter evinced a woefully inadequate grasp of the matter he was investigating.

"He referred to them as the New Prosthesis League," Barlow told the assembly, who howled with laughter. "He was looking for something called 'the ROM Code.' He didn't know what a ROM chip was, he didn't know what code was, he didn't know whether it had been stolen or what exactly had happened to whatever it was.

"And I realized that what I was looking at there was a microcosm of a whole set of things that could begin to happen with the government and society and computers. And it was just a little pinpoint of future shock that was going to blow up into something big and ugly if we weren't very careful about how it got managed.

"A few days later, I found out that this process was well under way in the Secret Service," Barlow continued. "They had come up with something called Operation Sun Devil and they were breaking into the homes of teenage kids, rousting them up in the middle of the night, coming along with guns, sledgehammers and, I assumed, no more knowledge of the situation than Agent Baxter had when he showed up in Pinedale, Wyoming."

"It's simply beyond the reach or grasp of 99.9% of the people today" Kapor added, "given the relative immaturity of the technology and the fact that there hasn't been a concerted effort made from within the industry and the academic research community to make the stuff usable. And if it's not made usable, there's going to be an increasing gulf between the information haves and the have-nots.

"That's what led us to the whole metaphor of the 'electronic frontier.' All of the good stuff that we know about is sufficiently difficult that only a few pioneers, some outlaws, maybe a few vigilantes, and early settlers, are comfortable.

"Out on the frontier, there aren't established laws or practices," Kapor continued. "We're making it up as we go along. But ultimately we've got to civilize the frontier. We have to allow ordinary folks to come and settle. We need to build the equivalent of railroads, because if we don't take the lead in doing it and it kind of happens by itself, it's probably not going to come out in a way that any of us really like it."

The Electronic Frontier Foundation began when Kapor, after reading an article Barlow had (on the WELL computer network) about his visit from Agent Baxter, visited Barlow in Wyoming one afternoon. "We realized that there was not so much a planned and concerted effort to subvert the Constitution," said Barlow, "as the natural process that takes place whenever there are people who are afraid and ignorant, and when there are issues that are ambiguous regarding Constitutional rights.

"Whenever there's a new medium, there's always a struggle to find out whether the Constitution is going to apply to that medium, whether or not the first amendment will apply. There's now a struggle under way to find out whether free speech can be expressed in bytes and bits. And that's basically what the Electronic Frontier Foundation is about.

"We're looking at a whole range of things dealing with future shock, the anxiety of society at large toward computers, the particular anxiety of society at large toward hackers, and what I like to call the learning curve of Sisyphus—which is what happens when you've got a technology that develops faster than anybody's ability to learn it."

Shortly after the EFF reception in Silicon Valley, R. U. Sirius and I met with Barlow and Kapor to learn more.

- David Gans

An Acid Take on Digital Capitalism

JOHN PERRY BARLOW: On May Day of this year, I got a phone call from FBI Agent Baxter down in Rock Springs. I said, "What do you want to talk to me about?" And he said, "I'll tell you when I get there. I've got a stack of papers." And he *did* have a stack of papers.

MONDO 2000: Wait a minute. So the FBI calls and says we need to see you...?
JPB: Well, yeah. That happens.

M2: And you thought it was neighborly to invite 'em over and hear 'em out?
JPB: Well, I thought it was probably closer to my best interests to do that then to tell him if he came I'd kill him.

So his stack of papers was about something called the NuPrometheus League, and they'd taken a little snippet of Apple's ROM code and had sent it to, among other people, Mitch Kapor. Understand that Apple basically sells ROM code. I mean, it's commonly thought to sell machinery, but what they really sell is the software that's on the ROM chip inside that machinery. That's the holy mojo that makes a Macintosh a Macintosh. So Apple freaked. And they invoked the awesome forces of the FBI which, for reasons having to do with corporate culture, is closely tied in with Apple's security company. There's a revolving-door policy between the FBI and Apple's security contractor.

M2: Mitch, the person or persons who call themselves the NuPrometheus League sent this piece of code out to a bunch of people, including yourself. Why did they do that and what was it?

MITCH KAPOR: I don't have the faintest idea why they sent it to me [laughter]. I just stuck the thing in the drawer, because it was an unlabeled diskette and I was afraid of viruses.

JPB: [laughing] A disk that says "Apple Source Code" on it, it's kind of like, [seductively] "Put me on your computer."

MK: But then the story hit the papers that somebody had actually taken a small, not terribly important piece of the source code for something called 8-bit color QuickDraw and sent it out. So I looked at it long enough to determine that it looked like Apple source code. Then I sent it back to Apple and thought that was the end of it. Several months later I got a call from the FBI. It was actually before John's visit.

M2: Did you guys already know each other?

JPB: Yeah. I'd interviewed Mitch for *MicroTimes*. We became friends in the first 30 seconds. It was one of those cosmic recognition experiences. Here was somebody else thinking some of the peculiar thoughts that I'd previously thought were mine alone... coming at it from a completely different angle.

MK: We're both interested in dislocations of consciousness because we think that's a central element to understanding how weird the world is— how everybody's mind has gotten genuinely bent, especially by technology... especially by digital media. John, of course, is in the process of writing a book about this.

We also had a common set of experiences in the '60s involving what I—when I speak to straight business audiences—charitably refer to as recreational chemicals, which contributed to a fundamental outlook ...

M2: Ye olde acid heads' league...

JPB: : Right! You got it, buster.

But *now* we're talking about that dislocation that occurs when an entire society looks up and finds that it doesn't know where it is, and it doesn't know how anything works anymore, and doesn't know how to deal with the reality that most of the standard, nurturing concepts that have managed to provide for us since the Neolithic Age—things like place and embodiment and community—are basically suddenly gone.

MK: I like John's one-sentence definition of cyberspace: "the place you are when you are on the telephone" It brings it home to people.

JPB: As a society, we're leaving the landscape and moving onto the map, without paying much attention to the process or the destination.

M2: Mitch, you've gone from being an acid head in the '60s to being one of the new heroes of digital capitalism. What's the view like from there?

MK: Well, before I was a digital capitalist, I taught meditation. Then I was a counselor in the psych unit of a local community hospital. I have a Master's degree in counseling psychology. So I've been pretty much all over the map. I just kind of fell into computers. I didn't set out to be Bill Gates. Bill Gates set out to be Bill Gates. My perspective wasn't shaped by needing to build a big company and make a lot of money. In a nutshell, I started this little company called Lotus and made this software product that several million people wound up buying. The little company turned into this enormous thing with thousands of employees making hundreds of millions of dollars a year. And it felt awful to me. So I left. I just walked away one day.

M2: Did it occur to you, when you walked away, that you were essentially turning

that large capitalist organism loose to do its will and...

JPB: It was already a lot bigger than he was.

M2: But if your values were offended by it, wasn't there some way to turn it around?

JPB: You're still stuck in the notion that people run these things and that they don't run themselves. Companies become their market, not their maker. Lotus is a beautiful case in point. So to say that Mitch could have somehow directed Lotus in some benign way is like assuming a coral polyp can run a reef. Large businesses are collective organisms.

M2: How are they driven?

MK: They're not! That's something that John and I keyed in on. We have this assumption that because something exists and acts, it has some central controller, some little homunculus inside it that makes the thing go. But physics is dead as a model for organization. Biology is in the ascendant. And if you study biology, things are very decentralized, very distributed. You get emergent behaviors coming out of the workings of a whole bunch of little pieces. Each piece is pretty dumb. Organizations are like that. Still and all, I agonized over my responsibilities toward Lotus before I left.

JPB: Individuals who work in institutions are no longer individuals. I mean, there's a big difference between a solitary wasp and a wasp's nest. It's like slime mold. Slime mold's basically like a paramecium-style, one-celled organism most of the time. When it decides that it wants to cover some country because conditions are changing, all the local slime molds get together and create an organism that grows stalks with eyes on the ends, and grows cilia to move with, and suddenly it's a critter.

M2: It's called "grexing."

JPB: Yeah! It's an animal then. It's no longer a one-celled organism. And then it goes someplace and devos. It goes back down to its original constituents. This is really the perfect metaphor for what a corporation is. And to say that the individuals inside that corporation are individuals when they're acting in their corporate form is like saying that slime mold is still a whole bunch of slime mold cells. We still have this sort of Newtonian, causal, deterministic notion that organizations are machines. The CEO is up in the wheel house and there's a direct connection between the chairman's desk and the rudder.

By the way, there's also this lingering assumption that there's some disjuncture between being a digital pioneer and being an acid head. It's my perception, on the basis of having interviewed a lot of the first wave, that this is actually quite a common phenomenon.

M2: In that case, is there a reaction of old corporate America against new corporate America?

JPB: Well, the reaction is to meet it, to infect it with itself, and to create—through the use of itself as a market—a perfect replica of what was preexisting.

M2: Apple is becoming like GM.

JPB: Oh, I think Apple's a lot worse than GM, because Apple is still clinging to a lot of mythology that just gets in the way. I mean, if Apple could just kind of settle in and be GM, everybody there would be a lot happier.

MK: It lacks the comfort and self-assurance of a mature organization which, no matter how much you might disagree with its values, has a certain degree of predictability. Younger organizations that are still in the throes of violent organizational psychoses become very unpredictable.

JPB: Apple is like the Chinese Cultural Revolution conducted by people in three-piece suits. Any corporation has a totalitarian quality, but people work for them because it's supposed to be safe, right? You give up your mind but get the benefit of the collective immune system that will protect you against the slings and arrows of individual fortune. So IBM takes care of their employees. They rarely fire anyone. They've got a nice retirement plan... they take care of their employees. Apple exercises much the same kind of totalitarian control over its employees and offers them *none* of the benefits. They have no retirement plan, period.

MK: Instead they offer up the vision that they're doing something to make a difference in the world, which *used* to be true.

M2: So who benefits?

JPB: That's kind of like saying, "What good are mosquitoes?" Mosquitoes arise because there's room for them in the ecology. Corporations arose because there was an ecological niche in the economy that was created by a lot of things, modern telecommunications being one.

M2: So Mitch, how did you end up thinking for yourself?

MK: I can't help it...

THE ORIGINS OF THE ELECTRONIC FRONTIER FOUNDATION

MK: I read John's account of his visit from Agent Baxter on the WELL, and it reverberated very deeply within me because it enabled me to begin to come to terms with a very disturbing experience that I hadn't been able to process. So I just sort of repressed it. It had sort of been lying in an undigested state in some empty chamber of my brain.

My experience was remarkably similar to John's. They were asking a lot of the same questions. It was hard work just getting them to understand the sequence of events I described here earlier. You know, "I had this diskette and I looked at it and I saw it was Apple source code and I sent it back. And *that* took a couple of hours to get across. It was exhausting. And I felt bad, because it was pretty clear to me that they weren't in a position
to do what they were supposed to be doing.

I sensed danger. When you have a powerful force with a charter and a history and they're fundamentally lost—they don't understand the territory they're in at all—it's a recipe for disaster.

JPB: Meanwhile, some other things had been happening that weren't directly connected to this case, but were certainly connected to the underlying cause. I had been part of an online *Harper's* magazine forum on computer hackers. In the course of this I'd met these cracker kids from New York and elsewhere. They were young and brash, and there had been a kind of nasty symmetry that set itself up over the course of the conference between the old techno-hippies and these young sort of digital skateboarders. It culminated in one of them downloading my TRW file with my credit history—with the implication that he could change it if he wanted to...

MK: Which wasn't true.

JPB: But I didn't know that. I was looking at life without credit. Pretty scary.

So I e-mailed this kid and I said, "We've just exceeded the bandwith of this medium. Why don't you give me a call? And I won't insult your intelligence by giving you my phone number." He called me about 20 minutes later.

The kid that I encountered on the phone was not at all the kid who'd been strutting about in full digital regalia on the WELL. He was a kid, you know? Smart, brash, New York street-kid, but not dissimilar from what I'd been at his age. And I got to know his colleagues. They were unquestionably inclined to trespass, but I tend to think that's sort of a testosterone-based endeavor that has long been with us.

I met them in New York, and I didn't find them to be any particular threat, in spite of their willingness to go where uninvited. But at a certain point I found out that the government had moved in on one of my young colleagues and had smashed down his door one afternoon while he was out and held his 12-year-old sister at gunpoint for an hour until he showed up.

I heard about this before I had my visit from the FBI and I thought, "Well, I don't know what they did. They're probably much worse than I thought." So I didn't do anything about it until I had the visit from the FBI.

MK: Yeah, and I came along and talked to John, also. I just thought that these kids should have a good lawyer. I saw that there were powerful forces moving against them. My sense of fairness dictated that they have adequate legal representation to protect their rights. That's where it started.

M2: What does this software multimillionaire feel in common with these "digital skateboarders?"

MK: You know, I'm the same digital skateboarder that they are, only I'm a little bit older and have more life experience. I was sort of a smart, nerdy, somewhat undersocialized kid. If I'd had the opportunity to do what they'd done, I probably would have done it.

JPB: A very important point that we have to make over and over and over again is that the Electronic Fronter Foundation is not a crackers' defense fund. Trespass is, and should be, against the law for a variety of reasons, not the least of which is that you could get in there and inadvertently create mayhem.

Robert Morris [creator of the Internet worm] is an excellent case in point. Morris wanted to do something that was really kind of cool. I wish he'd succeeded. He wanted to map the net. The Morris worm was like an explorer. It was going to go around to every node on the net and report back in and tell you just how big this sucker was. Which is something that nobody knows, right? It's a cool thing to do. Somebody ought to do it. Trouble is, he screwed up. His worm wasn't well-written, so the effect was viral rather than exploratory.

That's why it probably ought to be illegal to trespass. These people are entering into sensitive places where things are fragile. But it's also important that you don't go around busting joyriders for grand theft auto. Trying to impose a million-dollar fine and thirty years in jail on them just because they've trespassed digitally rather than physically is completely out of scale. That has to be dealt with.

M2: At the same time that your effort to bring rights and justice to the electronic frontier is happening, there's an immense tide of repression going on in all the old traditional realms and modes of communication.

JPB: No. If you check it out. you'll find that print and speech are still pretty well protected. Where you're running into trouble is every other medium. You're running into trouble with records, CDs, photographs, art, broadcast media, digital media...

We lost radio and television in the 20s and 30s... not a big civil libertarian time. They said, "Well, there's a limited amount of bandwidth so we've got to regulate it. And in regulating it, we've got to make certain that it meets the requirements of a wide audience."

M2: : Could the Electronic Frontier Foundation possibly step back a couple of decades and try to deal with that situation?

JPB: No, because of the way in which the legal system works. It's all organized by precedent. You build up a body of case law over a period of time and pretty soon it had the same authority as it would have if it were part of the Constitution. I don't think there's a damn thing we can do about the broadcast media now. And what scared Mitch and me is that we have cases that would establish the same kind of precedent-setting effect regarding digital media. So we'd have a fundamentally limited application of the Constitution to the world of bits and bytes. And if you think about it, it's *all* pretty much taking place now in bits and bytes, at some level of development. If you can restrict free speech just because it happens to occur in a magnetic medium, then it's all up for grabs.

M2: We're faced with the possibility that the Bill of Rights will be left behind with hot lead.

JPB: Much of the Bill of Rights is already gone. I was shocked to find out that the Fourth Amendment had had pretty much disappeared since the last time I'd looked. I called up these lawyers and said, "As I read the Fourth Amendment, this is unreasonable search and seizure to a tee." And they said, "Well, you've got to understand what's happened in terms of precedents on Fourth Amendment issues. We've basically lost it." It's the death of a thousand torts. We're still pursuing it though, because most of these Operation Sun Devil search warrants were unsigned, sealed, and completely broad. They just said, "Get everything that has electronics in it and get everything that has magnetism on it."

The Fourth Amendment is supposed to prevent the authorities from taking anything from you that doesn't have a direct instrumentality in the alleged crime. So they know what a gun is, right? But they don't know what a computer virus is or where it might reside in 25,000 disks, so they take them all.

A NEW MARKET FOR THE SECRET SERVICE

JPB: The Secret Service wants to expand into a new market. The old market—which contrary to popular belief wasn't protecting presidents, it was busting counterfeiters—moved offshore. So in order to have a reason to exist as an organization with a budget—to feed itself as a critter—they had to find some new food. They've gone into computer crime and they're doing a rather bad job of it. They're getting terrible advice from the telcos, who are using the Secret Service in much the same way that the FBI is being used by Apple. If you call the telcos and ask them a question about computer crime, you'll find yourself talkin' to somebody from the Secret Service. The Secret Service agents showed up at all these busts with telco security people. You couldn't tell them apart.

See, the government is now grinding to a complete halt, and what's actually running stuff—to the extent that things are getting run—is corporations. They're mediating the economy. They're passing the goods and services around. And they're doing all the control stuff, they're managing the consciousness, and now they're moving into law enforcement.

M2: That's very much the cyberpunk view.

JPB: Yeah, exactly.

CHAPTER THREE: CLOWN PRINCE OF THE DIGITAL REVOLUTION

R.U. Sirius Guide to the Alternative '70s (bOING bOING, 1993)

Kathy Acker: Where Does She Get Off? an Interview (io, 1993)

Pomo to Go: a User's Guide to Trendy French Intellectuals (With Carmen Hermosillo, Wired 1994)

Cyberpunk Lite: William Gibson Waxes Laconic —an Interview (Unpublished, 1994)

The Tyranny of H... (21•C, 1995)

A Guy With a Backache: R.U. Sirius interviewed by 01 (1995)

THIS IS MY TOENAIL..GET IT!

Introduction to Chapter 3

You don't appreciate the good times while you're in them. When I decided to "go solo," I thought there was a good chance that I would get my own TV show, at the very least. If not that, surely some well-financed magazine would want me as an Editor-In-Chief. A lucrative speaking tour was a *sure shot* according to the lecture agent that Howard Rheingold introduced me to. Book contracts would be like shooting ducks in a barrel. Ha!

So by the light of my superstar expectations, this period was a disappointing drag. But it was, at least up until this point, my period of peak earnings as a freelance writer. I cranked out mediocre monthly columns in my sleep for foreign magazines ranging from *Japan Esquire* to *Wave* (published out of Amsterdam) and did some better work for *Wired* and *21•C*. I didn't worry about the magazines published in foreign languages too much because I couldn't *read* them anyway, and I knew the interpretative process would render them ridiculous anyway. (When you're already on the borderline of ridiculous, a foreign interpretation pushes you over the edge). After all, I'd had an article about me in a Japanese magazine interpreted for me while I was at *MONDO*. The article said that I went into my backyard every night and watched *Tetsuo* on a big screen, a glorious image worthy of Coppola at the very least, but I have no idea how they got that out of anything I said.

After whipping up a proposal for the first technoculture TV show, *Sirius Television,* with John Sanborn and the gang at Colossal/Big Pictures *(Liquid Television, Aeon Flux)*, and having it nearly picked up by PBS, only to be dropped, and then ripped off and watered down by a Colossal/Tartikoff alliance (and it *still* never sold), and flirting around about a more commercial Fox-TV-oriented pitch with Propaganda Films and Brett Leonard *(Lawnmower Man, Virtuosity)* that also never grew legs, I finally scored a record deal and a book contract, sort of.

MONDO Vanilli met Trent Reznor at a party at the ol' Tate mansion, scene of Mansonoid horror back in '69, where he was living. MONDO Vanilli's main musician, Scrappi DüChamp, proffered an MV demo tape on the Trentster. He *loved* it. Of course, he had eaten a few magic mushrooms at the party, but his enthusiasm hadn't diminished when he visited us in San Francisco. The rest of it is a long sad tale. Mr. Disappointment, true to his song lyrics, let us down. MONDO Vanilli's *IOU Babe,* unreleased by Nothing Records although recorded on their dime ($90,000 actually) still lies in wait (at http://www.scrappi.com/ioualbum)

While we were recording *IOU Babe,* former *MONDO* Senior Editor St. Jude and I were writing *How to Mutate and Take Over the World* for Ballantine Books... Disappointment #2 would hit as we rolled into 1996 and *Mutate* didn't sell, and was ignored by the media—both digital and mainstream—and by our pals in the cyber-elite

These two pieces, *IOU Babe* and *HTM&TOW* had some things in common. They both had a nasty undertow to them. The ideas and emotions they were attempting to evoke were not available on their surfaces. And the surfaces themselves were abrasive. And they weren't constructed to appeal to anything that anybody would particularly be looking for, in a book or in a record. By the time *Mutate* failed in 1996, I nursed an extreme and unhealthy resentment towards audiences, consumers, reviewers, journalists, the arts and entertainment industries... human beings in general. This bitter disgust informed the best writing of my career, which you won't find in *this* chapter, but in the first one... in my REVOLTING! period. But you can see the beginnings of the REVOLTING! sensibility in here. Just imagine my wheels spinning in a void and a prolonged howl of frustration and bile slowly rising up in my throat. spinning in a void and a prolonged howl of frustration and bile slowly rising up in my throat.

R.U. Sirius' Guide to the Alternative '70s

bOING bOING #12, 1993

Nostalgia sucks. All us cool people agree. On the other hand, as life in the nineties becomes increasingly more demented and unlivable, even you might find yourself pining for a time when the appropriate-dress issue in high school was whether boys should be allowed to wear mascara, and not whether girls should be allowed to carry an AK, or if a handgun should suffice.

So they're repackaging the seventies for us. And they're doing it with a knowing, doesn't-this-make-you-wanna-puke nudge 'n' wink. But this ol' fart wants to let you genx brats in on a little secret: The seventies actually were cool. Much cooler than the ballyhooed sixties. There was more sex in the seventies, more tolerance, the right wing was completely in retreat, Richard Nixon was still a pig, and cocaine wasn't bad for your health yet! In the mid-seventies it was possible to believe that the whole country was moderately hip — and if that wasn't enough, Punk was coming along to kick moderately hip's laidback butt.

So how did we get from a time when lipstick boys smoked pot in the White House with the Republican President's son while Secret Service agents smiled on... to a time when wanting to fuck a teenager is more horrible than lobbing some intelligent bombs at foreigners? How did we get from a time when the biggest problem was lame 5-minute guitar solos on the radio to a time when the Reverend Wildmon rules the airwaves? I know you've been asking yourself just these questions. Which is why I'm gonna now letcha know just how we blew it, back in **the seventies**

1970–1971:
The Time is Right for Fighting in the Streets, Boy... er – Womyn!

Pass out the guns and ammo
We're gonna blast our way through here
We've got to get together sooner or later
Because the revolution's here
And you know that it's right
– "Something In The Air" by Thunderclap Neumann, #1 on the hit parade during the summer of '71

The '60s started in 1964 when the Beatles toured America and ended in 1972 with the re-election of President Nixon, and the realization that Yippies and motley longhaired ultraleftists just couldn't get tens of thousands of youngsters into the streets to burn down banks and throw rocks at pigs anymore. But to understand the early '70s, you've

first got to look at the late '60s. For all the media hype about the '60s, more than half of the high school and college-age kids were still living in the '50s in the '60s. They started living in the '60s in 1969, and continued living there through the early '70s. Got it?

Listen. In 1968, a Beatles song, "The Ballad of John and Yoko," was banned by most radio stations because it had the word "Christ" in it, for Christ's sake. OK, maybe they actually banned it because everybody hated Yoko, but the point still sticks—you just couldn't catch the Butthole Surfers on MTV in those fabulous hippie years.

But something kind of cool happened right around '69. I saw it at my high school (Binghamton NY Central). In '67–'68, everybody wanted to kill us freeks (Hippies thought the hippie image was too wimpy even back then, ya punks... We called ourselves freeks instead... which now means girls who like to fuck. Stop snickering, punk—you wanna know what punk used to mean?). Suddenly in 1969, everybody was a freek. Guys who were punching me out for my anti-war buttons last year were wearing Che Guevara T-shirts.

Anyway, 1970-1971... there were over 500 anti-establishment bombings nationwide. There were riots on every single major college campus in America. The Bank of America on Isla Vista was torched and the happy students toasted marshmallows on it, yes they did. Eldridge Cleaver's exiled Black Panther chapter, the Weather Underground, the Yippies, and Timothy Leary all together announced an American government-in-exile in Algiers

Anyway, you get the picture. To understand the early '70s, consider the fact that generational unity was so casually accepted that Alice Cooper could sing about "us" in a way that even Fugazi wouldn't touch in these cynical and decentralized times...

We've still got a long way to go
What's keeping us apart isn't selfishness
What's holding us together isn't love
– "We've Still Got A Long Way to Go" by Alice Cooper, from Love it to Death, 1971

Speaking of Alice, his Love it to Death and David Bowie's Space Oddity may have announced the start of the actual seventies.

1972–1974: Walk on the Wild Side

Maybe it was the release of Andy Warhol's book, The Philosophy of Andy Warhol from A to B and Back Again, (but then again maybe it wasn't, since I can't remember for sure when that book was released.) Either way, 1972–1974 saw the first hip rebellion against hippies and the pressures of political correctness.

It was called glam or glitter, and if you believe the persisting rumors that it was lame, go back and listen to the records. Killer and Billion Dollar Babies by Alice Cooper. Transformer and Berlin by Lou Reed. Hunky Dory, The Rise and Fall of Ziggy Stardust, and Aladdin Sane by the master of the zeitgeist, Bowie. Electric Warrior and Slider by T Rex. Stranded by Roxy Music. Mott by Mott the Hoople. New York Dolls' first album. After years on acid, drinking beer was a mind-blowing revelation. After endless sucking up to the lesbian Kim Il Sung faction in prolewear, what a joy to string on Mom's jewelry and head for the town gay bar. Yup, even in backwater Binghamton, the hip thing to do in the glam era was hang in gay bars. Even Dylan wore rouge!

OK, so the platforms were tacky, pretentiousness was *de rigueur,* and Bowie caused the eventual outbreak of Suede. At least this first post-hippie boho revolt didn't dote day-in-day-out on the karma of Being There Then and the revolutionary significance of Health Food Collectives! Sheesh: ya had to be there... then.

1974-1976: The Fall of America #1.0

Nixon Resigns! America Loses The Vietnam War! The Hippies Were Right! No exaggera tion. The Watergate hearings shocked the empire temporarily to its senses. Try to understand that this was still a time when "the whole nation" might all actually be focused on the same "matters of significance," and the "silent majority" still held precious the illusion that we were a "free" country and not just a powerful one. Revelations of lies and manipulation of the allegedly free press raged across the media. It ranged from the big lie that turned the Vietnam "conflict" into a raging fullscale war, to the use of police-state tactics and intelligence agencies for every- thing from spying on dissenters, to the most trivial personal agenda items of a raving paranoid president. So Nixon resigned and the US withdrew from Vietnam as victori- ous commies paraded through Saigon. It was, in the words of the still-vital William S. Burroughs, "the fall of America's Image Capital."

For a period of about five years, the right wing and its supposedly-silent major- ity actually shut the fuck up. Actors saluted the Viet Cong while accepting Oscars, with barely a peep from the Bob Hope/Frank Sinatra axis. Even my cousin Peter's conservative father started letting him smoke pot and snort coke at home. There was—if not less certainty than there is today — less enforcement of the pretense of certainty.

America sort of shrugged its shoulders in the mid-'70s and said the hippies were right. The hippies shrugged their shoulders as well. They hadn't yet realized that, with pot four times as strong, the daily morning joint would make them forget to get out of bed till evening. Into this vacuum came the malaise-wonks, Jimmy Carter and Jerry Brown, telling the dazed American public what to expect. NOTHING!

Nothing except great fucking energetic rock and roll coming out of New York City. Patti Smith. The Ramones. Talking Heads. Richard Hell. Television. Blondie. To be on the NY club scene in '75–'76 was to transcend the political moment for a musical trend that was peculiar in a way that no rock trend before or since has come close to matching.

1977–1978: No Future!

The Sex Pistols, of course, blew everything away in 1977. Here in the oh-so-self- aware '90s, we wander zombie-like amongst the shards, muttering about dysfunctionality and co-dependence, and life as only a stay of execution. In a "dead pan" world where the digitized records of our existence take precedence over spontaneous, energized, eroticized living, we work to build the machines that will displace us. But it sure was a cool way to end history; with Rotten as the prophet, Vicious-the-hippy's-kid as the human sacrifice and McLaren selling the souvenirs.

1979–Present: America Held Hostage

Here in the '90s, in the Afternoon of the Living Dead, the real world is just like tabloid TV. The police state lurches on, throwing only the occasional downsized war, hardwiring the datascape, perfecting the politics of simulation and perceptual engineering. Now that her citizens are blank slates, defined by what we've quit doing, we're ready to be sold a redigitized dub of that decade of polyester and mindless hedonism, the SEVENTIES. Yeah, dude, hit it:

Whether you're a mother
Or whether you're a brother
You're just stayin' alive, stayin' alive
Inner city breakin' up
And everybody's shaken
But we're stayin' alive, stayin' alive huh huh huh, stayin' alive.

– Feel-good sounds from those cocaine-addicted chipmunks, the Bee Gees: Saturday Night Fever

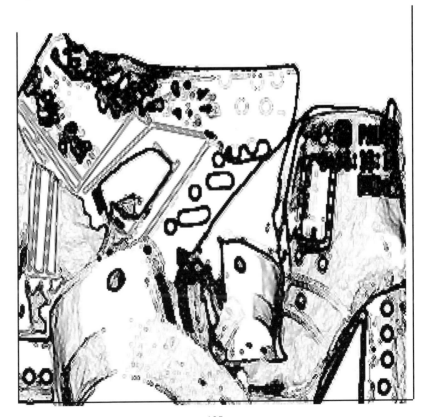

135

Kathy Acker: Where Does She Get Off?

io, **1993**

She calls herself Acker. And Acker is this person I hang with sometimes. What's cool is that we can talk about anything and nobody gets uptight (though she does decide that I'm a sexist pig sometimes). Some have called her the next generation's Burroughs. Kathy Acker is a novelist. I first read her interior staccato noise in a Canadian Dadaist magazine sometime in the late 1970s. I thought, "Here's the next generation's Burroughs." Or something like that. She uses appropriation, multiple points-of-ego, multiple points-in-time, honest and violent libidinal obsessions, deconstructionist discourse and revolutionary disgust to great advantage. Her books include *Blood and Guts in High School, Empire of the Senseless, In Memoriam to Identity* and most recently, *My Mother: Demonology.* She lives in San Francisco and teaches at the San Francisco Art Institute.

Kathy Acker: So this is like a serious interview ...

Sirius: Yeah, this is a literary magazine, only cooler. I was reading *In Memoriam to Identity* — that part about a woman who's encouraged by a professor to poison somebody ...

KA: *Don Quixote?*

RU: Uh ...

KA: I don't remember. I write it to get it out of me. I don't write it to remember it.

RU: OK. Enough about books. Let's talk about the wild girls. Are they on your mind?

KA: (laughs) The students who come to my class are very closely related to all the evil girls who are very interested in their bodies and sex and pleasure. I learn a lot from them about how to have pleasure and how cool the female body is. One of my students had a piercing through her labia. And she told me about how when you ride on a motorcycle, the little bead on the ring acts like a vibrator. Her story turned me on so I did it. I got two. It was very cool.

I'm very staid compared to my students, actually. I come from a generation where you've got the PC dikes and confused heterosexuals. No one ever told me that you could walk around with a strap-on, having orgasms.

RU: That's one of the things I find interesting about your writing. You seem to write from the point of orgasm — but you stretch it out. It's the kind of interior dialogue you might have during extreme arousal. How do you do that?

KA: Well, I think writing is basically about time and rhythm. Like with jazz. You have your basic melody and then you just riff off of it. And the riffs are about timing. And about sex. Writing for me is about my freedom. When I was a kid, my parents were like monsters to me, and the world extended from them. They were horrible. And I was this good little girl — I didn't have the guts to oppose them. They told me what to do and how to be. So the only time I could have any freedom or joy was when I was alone in my room. Writing is what I did when I was alone with no one watching me or telling me what to do. I could do whatever I wanted. So writing was really associated with body pleasure—it was the same thing. It was like the only thing I had.

Rolfing the "I"

KA: I've been going to this Rolfer. I don't know why I'm doing it. It's like: "You will get rid of all your childhood traumas if you only go through this pain." Fuck childhood. People always say you do all these things because of your childhood. I'm sorry, but what really gets me off is the idea that you can just travel, and traveling is just like having an endless orgasm. You just go and go and go.

RU: In that state, you lose your individual identity — and therefore your childhood. But the Rolfer is trying to drag you back into accepting your singular identity.

KA: Yeah. He's telling me, "Your agenda is ..." and I'm saying, "My agenda? I don't have an agenda and I'm not sure who I am. Who am I?" He keeps on saying, "You know what you want." And I say, "I don't know what I want."

RU: If he succeeds in dragging you into a singular "I," that's the death of Kathy Acker the writer.

KA: Yeah, it sure is. But I don't think he'll succeed. He doesn't have a fuckin' chance. I'm just trying to fuck him. If he won't fuck, we're not going anywhere. He can't make me into this singular "I." I told him, "You gotta consider the pleasure principle—namely my pleasure." He didn't like that.

RU: I always say, divide the word "therapist" between the "e" and the "r."

KA: Yeah. The rapist. Because they're taking all your childhood wonderment and reducing it to childhood trauma. He gives me these long lectures about how he's not enlightened and he wants to be an animal. Can you imagine long lectures about wanting to be an animal? What a fuckin' bozo!

RU: When I was in college, all of the poetry teachers worshipped Robert Bly, so I had my fill of that shit.

KA: I told him about my piercings and he said, "Oh, you're a wild woman." Then I asked him if he wanted to see my piercings. He wouldn't do it.

Piercing the Kundalini

RU: As for the piercings and all that — do you like the term "modern primitive?"

KA: I thought it [the RE/Search book, Modern Primitives] was kind of kinky at the time. I wasn't really into body piercings until I found that about half my female students had them. And then I thought, "What is this about?"

RU: Everybody around the Bay Area seems to be into it.

KA: Well, you know why — you get high as hell!

RU: But you don't have to make permanent changes to your body to get high. There has to be more to it.

KA: We're not just talking high. I mean, I thought they would just be like sex toys and they're really pretty. I didn't know I would get that high. First of all, during the piercings they told me, "Breathe like this. Ground yourself and do really deep breathing. And if you do it right, the kundalini will come. The energy will go right to the top

137

of your brain and shoot out." And it did!

Then I went to a bar and started to come. And I just kept coming. I still haven't totally come down yet. I don't know how it effects everybody else, but what it did to my body was totally open up some kind of sex chakra.

RU: Does part of the high come from the awareness of having permanently changed the body?

KA: Yeah, it's being in the world with a different — I don't know exactly. I'm still learning. It's like I suddenly have a cock. There's something always there, and I can feel it. It's like a totally new experience of being female. A friend told me that there are these clean and sober dykes that have piercings every couple months just to get high. It's about learning about my body. I didn't know my body could do this. It's not exactly pleasure. It's more like vision. I didn't know the body is such a visionary factory. Basically we grew up not wanting to know that we had bodies. And it's not as if these piercings are in that deep — it's just on the surface. So if that little thing can do so much, who knows what else we can experience?

WRITING ...

RU: Uh, shouldn't we be talking about writing?

KA: Oh yeah, writing. It's a literary magazine.

RU: Yeah, writing (long pause). Part of your recent novel, *My Mother: Demonology*, was based on some stuff by Bataille. Why did you pick Bataille?

KA: Bataille's cool!

RU: I can't get into him. In fact, I'm writing a piece for *Wired* called "A User's Guide to Trendy French Intellectuals" that thoroughly trashes all those people.

KA: Oh, evil person! You're so dumb, man. They're cool.

RU: So tell me about Bataille.

KA: Bataille is associated with the surrealists. Basically the idea is that democracy doesn't work. Communism doesn't work. All these fucking models aren't working. We've got to find some new models — a model of what society should look like.

We don't know what humans are like. And the ground is not economics; it's not like people do everything they do for economic reasons. You've got to look at the imagination; you've got to look at sex. We have no way of describing these things using the language we have. So a group was formed around Bataille to try to figure out what it means to be human — what society should look like. Humans have to live in a society — they can't just survive as individuals. That's not a viable condition. You know, everyone's always talking about trauma and pain and how this society isn't working, that we shouldn't have racism and sexism, but we never talk in positive terms — like what joy would be, what it would be like to have a totally great existence. Bataille and his followers looked for models for people to have totally great existences.

RU: What did they come up with?

KA: Well, they looked at tribal models and how they dealt with sexual stuff and sacrifice and property — the joys that aren't based on economic accumulation and the workaday world, but based on giving it all up — not having that specific, controlling, imprisoning "I." He wasn't a Freudian. He was much more interested in the tribal model where everything is on the surface and you deal with sexual stuff the same way you deal with economic stuff and social stuff. He was a very proper person, a librarian. Bataille's main enemy was Jean Paul Sartre — Bataille wasn't an upper-class intellectual and he took a lot of pressure because of that. Sartre wrote this really horrible article about Bataille and sort of kept his work from getting recognized.

RU: When you sit down to write, do you empty your mind to see what comes up?
KA: Lately I've been working on narrative, so I don't do it that way now. But I'm starting to worry about self-censorship — that I might be internalizing some shit. I might be writing what people expect me to write, writing from that place where I might be ruled by economic considerations. To overcome that, I started working with my dreams, because I'm not so censored when I use dream material. And I'm working at trying to find a kind of language where I won't be so easily modulated by expectation. I'm looking for what might be called a body language. One thing I do is stick a vibrator up my cunt and start writing — writing from the point of orgasm and losing control of the language and seeing what that's like.

Vanity Scare
KA: We're being really serious like we're doing an interview for a literary magazine, but have you seen the *Vanity Fair* issue with Roseanne Barr on the cover? I haven't read the interview but — whoa! Those pictures are heavy! You know, everybody's screaming about PC on campuses and there's Roseanne spreading her legs.

RU: I didn't know anything about her until I saw one of those MTV "Year in Review" specials about three years ago. They had a bunch of people talking about what the year was like, and everybody was anti-establishment to one degree or another. They had Frank Zappa and Lou Reed and William Gibson, but Roseanne was the most radical. She was calling for armed revolution. I thought that she was part of some new revolutionary movement and somebody told me, "No, she's a television star."
KA: She's radical! I mean, I have respect for some of these Hollywood girls! Also, when you think about the holy trinity, Michael Jackson, Madonna and Roseanne — American culture is pretty cool. I mean, Michael Jackson is out there.

RU: Did you see his press conference? It was like the appearance of the Joker in *Batman*. I mean, the guy comes out to declare his innocence of so-called acts of perversion in this wild makeup and lipstick! The top entertainer in the world ...
KA: Talk about cyber-identity! It isn't like an older man having sex with a young boy — it's like a Martian having sex with a human.

RU: I admire Michael Jackson for his utter freakishness.
KA: Oh man, talk about body manipulation. He'll never come clean about it. I mean, does he get off on all of this? Does he get high from every bit of surgery?

RU: He's really going after being a proto-post-human of some sort. It's the first real-life Cronenberg horror movie. It's too bad that his words don't really express any of that.
KA: His lyrics are dumb.

RU: Bowie was brilliant at expressing otherness with his lyrics. Jackson is lame on that level. But what he actually does is so much more freakish.

139

KA: It's so rad, it beats Madonna silly. She has possibilities, but ...
RU: ... we need to talk to that girl.

GRRRLS WITH COCKS

RU: We've got to do something about this San Francisco wild girl scene. It's like Burroughs' wild boys turned out to be wild girls! I think there's something here that's even cooler than Riot Grrrls. Riot Grrrls are really PC.

KA: Oh, everybody knows that you're a sexist pig, R.U. Bikini Kill is cool! When I was in Seattle, this group had me judge a poetry reading contest and pick out somebody to do a reading with me. So there's this really cute, hot girl. So I said, "Yeah, man, her!" I asked her, "What are you doing poetry for? You should start a band." So she started Bikini Kill. She was cool. But Tribe 8 is really rad. It's way beyond Bikini Kill. I mean, for years we've had all this feminist crap of "It's not fair" or "We want the power," and here comes along some girls who don't give a shit, don't dislike men, have a good time and are for total revolution — and also, like, "We've got cocks too!"

I mean, packing is gonna make a major revolution! And the only thing guys have to learn is that there's nothing wrong with dicks and cocks, but don't think you've got the only cocks in the world.

RU: I've always advocated replaceable parts.

KA: Girls packing are so sexy. And girls going down on girls. Every man's gonna get off on seeing some girl packing — and every girl's gonna get off. I saw this video that teaches girls how to ejaculate. So now we can just come on some guy's face and say, "Eat it! Smudge it in."

RU: I guess that covers writing then.

KA: Right.

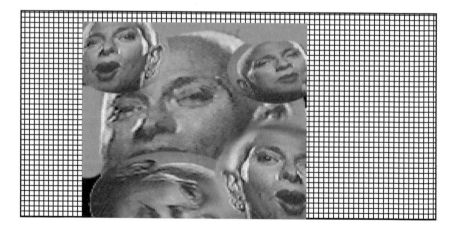

140

Pomo To Go:
A Usuers Guide To Trendy French Intellectuals

Co-authored with Carmen Hermosillo   *Wired,* **June 1994**

Pol Pot was educated in Paris. Years later, back home in Cambodia, he ordered his Khmer Rouge to execute all people with glasses—part of his war against intellectualism. Was Pol Pot's hostility displaced, an irritation, shared by so may, with the convoluted thought processes and obfuscatory language peculiar to *French* intellectuals? The latter seems, at least, a good guess.

Don't get me wrong. I have a soft spot for French writers. Back in my college days, I would argue with the fans of Spanish-language surrealists like Frederico Garcia Lorca and Gabriel Garcia Marquez. Sure, the Latins were deeper, more subtle, better writers. But those original dada guys, Breton and Tsara—blithely tossing firecrackers of dense language, contradictory words striking against one and other in paroxysms of pleasurable non sense— now that's what I call an afternoon's fun.

Torturing language certainly predates De Sade. Indeed, we can trace that French quality of huffiness all the way back to Voltaire. Or take Sartre, *please.* Only a Frenchman could come up with a philosophy of complete individual freedom and responsibility and use it to justify Maoism. (American college students in the 1960s don't really count in this regard. We're talking elegantly-languaged philosophy here, not youthful rituals of self-righteousness.) I don't know whether Mr. Pot shared *vin et fromage* with the nauseous one, or if he preferred the more violent thinker, M. Jean Genet.

But this is all old news. The big names now are Deleuze, Derrida, Baudrillard, and Kristeva; the fab four of post-modernism. Generally, the French PoMo thinkers succeed at two things: They offer a hysterical (read paranoid) but insightful perspective on the cruel and schizophrenic nature of late 20th century technoculture; and they engage in linguistic sophistry to try to save Marxism's irrelevant ass. Trendy French thinkers deal with language and reality in techno-terms; in other words, they view it all as a big machine or a complex system. And they therefore exert great influence on the cybercrit (genus academia) segment of cyberculture.

Reading any of these guys is exhausting, and it takes valuable time away from watching television advertising, which generally communicates the pomo experience with that American kind of immediacy that we all crave—even when it's on behalf of Trendy French Perfumes. This is why I'm providing you with this handy guide to trendy French Intellectuals. Quicker and easier even than *Monarch Notes,* this guide will give you enough information to banter in hip academic circles and, believe me, quoting Lacan can get you laid.

Let's start with some historically influential French thinkers. You need to know them because even though they are not directly related to the philosophies of postmodern discourse, they influenced the guys in the latter half of this guide—the really trendy ones.

Voltaire:

Voltaire was the icon-at-large and philosopher-punk of the Age of Reason. He's best known for his tale *Candide,* which expressed his contempt for those among his contemporaries who denied the existence of evil. Voltaire was an original flamer, creating that top note of bitchiness without which the arrogance of French philosophy would have been impossible. He offended so many people during his career that most people were surprised he died of natural causes, in his old age.

De Sade:

Working from his first-hand experience of the French aristocracy and the French Revolution, the Marquis de Sade used dense and darkly beautiful language, heavy with irony and sexual reference, to express his conviction that life was absurd. He spent 27 years in various states of imprisonment and detention in French prisons and castles as a result. He is, along with Lucifer and Aleister Crowley, one of the West's most mythic Bad Boys.

Baudelaire, Rimbaud, Verlaine, and *les Symbolistes*

The French Symbolists of the 19th century took the "elegantly wasted" decadence of British fops like Coleridge and supplemented it with the language of romantic hysteria. The speed and jumpiness of these poets predates and predicts the cut-ups of William S. Burroughs and the dense language of Spasm culture *a la* Arthur Kroker. Rimbaud's oft-quoted "intentional disordering of the senses" inspired the likes of Keith Richards and Patti Smith in more modern times. Today, after the H-bomb, LSD, MTV, and VR, we find even the most poetic among postmodern youth longing for a *re*ordering of the senses. Ain't gonna happen, son.

Tsara and Breton:

These two were among those who created the Dadaist and Surrealist movements. The Dadaists were this century's original media jammers, specializing in public acts of irrationality, scandal and confusion. Dadaism eventually became surrealism. The surrealists agreed with Freud that human consciousness, like an iceberg, lies mostly invisible beneath the surface. Surrealism attempted to explore the hidden areas of human consciousness through strange juxtapositions of words and images. As such, surrealism is a favorite reference point for both the psychedelic and multimedia cultures.

Duchamp:

Marcel Duchamp—inventor of modern appropriation in the form of the ready-made— changed the way the West sees art by showing that art is more likely to come from the eye of the artist than from the artist's hands. In other words, he demonstrated that artistic vision is more important than technical mastery. An elegant and quiet man, Duchamp is now honored in the art world, referenced by appropriationist collage artists like Negativland and John Oswald and *blamed* for Jeff Koons.

Jean Paul Sartre:

Jean-Paul Sartre was an existentialist. That means that he took atheism seriously. Atheism implies that there are no divine laws. If there are no divine laws then what you do is totally up to you and your desires and needs. Conversely, whatever happens to you is totally your own problem: The consequences of your choices are your personal responsibility. Somehow, in spite of this, he positioned himself 180 degrees to the left of Ayn Rand and Nietzche. Imagine yourself dead. Your consciousness is completely annihilated, you have ceased to exist and you will never ever exist again. This is death as the existentialist imagines it. Enjoy!

Genet:

George Bataille said of Jean Genet that he "chose to explore Evil as others have chosen to explore Good." Jean-Paul Sartre saw Genet as a saint. His romanticized view of the thief and the criminal was Americanized by Norman Mailer in the seminal 1950's beat-attitude essay, "The White Negro," and may have ultimately lead to a culture of Oliver North and Snoop Doggy Dogg. I leave it to you to fill in the blanks.

Debord and the Situationists

Guy Debord was the spokesman for the Situationists International, social critics who, in the 1960s, were the first to suggest that *image* was the real commodity in our society and that image would replace more traditional goods in the economy in the future. To understand image as commodity, just consider the entire world of television—from the network's corporate logo to the pr department — from the advertisers conflating their every product with sex, to the stars, their PR firms, and the gossip industry that makes them who we think they are. Also consider the consumer of television images and what he or she is purchasing from the couch. The Situationist concept of the "society of the spectacle"—in which living is replaced by viewing—maps perfectly to our culture of virtuality. The Situationist philosophy allies closely with the notion of false consciousness as preached by Herbert Marcuse, and they might be considered partly responsible for the smug superiority and intolerance of today's politically correct.

Bataille:

George Bataille was a French novelist and critic whose ideas very much influenced post-modern thinking about sexual politics and eroticism. In one of his most interesting collections of essays, *Literature and Evil*, Bataille argues for the primacy of what he calls "powerful communication" which he defines as privileged moments of supreme awareness based on emotions of sensuality, drama, love, separation, and death. In short, Bataille makes explicit the French intellectual's partly repressed tendency to be a drama queen.

Roland Barthes:

Roland Barthes' early work suggests that literature, in the traditional sense of the word, used language in the service of class divisions. (There. I just saved you from reading a few million words, most of them adjectives.) But the idea that traditional language excludes exploited classes has unfortunately led to the attempt to alter language by foisting incomprehensible replacements on college students. Among them, the works of Roland Barthes. Barthes also felt that authentic modernist literature would have to testify to its own ideological guilt. His point of view was well-articulated by Bataille when he said "Literature is not innocent." This was adopted by Sex Pistols' memetician Malcolm McLaren as "No one is innocent." You will note that M. Barthes didn't volunteer his own guilty ass for imprisonment or execution.

Baudrillard:
Jean Baudrilliard is a social theorist who has made his living explaining the emergence of mass culture and the increasing importance of social images as commodities—very much in the vein of the Situationists. To get a feel for the Baudrillardian "social-image-as-a-commodity," consider the term "spin doctor"; listen to Michael Jackson's lawyers, or examine the difference between a television commercial and a PBS "pledge break." Baudrillard talks about the regression of simulacra, the media hall-of-mirrors in which any reference to the actual disappears. Mick Jagger talked about the same thing 20 years ago in the film *Performance,* only he was in a bubble bath with the still-attractive Anita Pallenberg and an underaged androgynous French Girl. Baudrillard isn't *that* much fun, though he's the most popular trendy Frenchman with the college crowd.

Deleuze and Guattari:
In their ongoing attack on the theories of Freud, Gilles Deleuze and Felix Guatarri have proposed something called "schizoanalysis" as an alternative to psychoanalytic practice. They said, "A schizophrenic going for a walk is healthier than a neurotic on a couch," a philosophy that we find in practice on the streets of Berkeley, California. Scholars influenced by these two have recently raised the banner of cyberpunk science fiction, since the genre speaks directly to the schizoid character of techno/media life.

Jacques Derrida
Jacques Derrida is a philosopher concerned with the act of reading. He sees the scholar as a kind of priest and sees criticism and analysis as a kind of religious ritual performed upon a text. This makes Derrida very popular among academics, who would otherwise feel *completely* irrelevant in our media apocalypse. Recently, even academics have described Derrida's thinking as out of date. Derrida's progeny however, such as the brilliant Avital Ronell, have made it their business to read *technology* and the meaning of technoculture. The results are overwrought... but amusing.

Foucault:
Michel Foucault explored and analyzed the political and bureaucratic aspects of control and punishment. He was among the first to recognize and define our emerging technocratic surveillance culture in terms of the "panopticon," a multitiered prison complex in which all activity can be viewed by the overseers. Poor Michel. He didn't know about anonymous remailers.

Kristeva:
Julia Kristeva explores the place of the female in the patriarchy, or dominant social order. Like the American novelist Kathy Acker, she questions the whole idea of identity and asserts that the feminine has been marginalized and identified as Other. Other(ness) is a major buzzword in pomo feminist and minority discourse these days. For instance, female sexuality, in Western European culture, is frequently portrayed as a mysterious commodity with an aura that can be easily transferred to an artifact and purchased by the consumer. Americans have vulgarized this exotic romanticism to the point of unintentional parody by associating, for instance, bad beer with buxom bimbos. The only mystery, finally, is how anyone can be that stupid.

Lyotard:
Jean Francois Lyotard looks at what he calls "narrative," the idea that through language we tell ourselves stories about life, stories that have an internal logic and structure. He compares this with *scientific* language, which sees itself as superior to narrative language because it requires "scientific proof." Lyotard shows how scientific language eventually becomes a self-validating narrative itself through philosophical and political consensus. Science tells itself that scientific thought will ultimately end in the emancipation of humanity through Progress. This, according to Lyotard, is a crock of shit.

Lacan
Jacques Lacan did for philosophy and language what the Residents did for music. The Residents placed a high value on obscurity. Lacan placed a high value on the difficulty people had understanding his language. If you're unfamiliar with the Residents, then this may be a Lacanian discourse of sorts. Lacan said things like "language points to a lack" which apparently means that if you're talking about it, you're not getting any. And you thought the French were always at it! Quoting Lacan might score you the most points in post-modern intellectual circles. The reason for this remains—of course—obscure.

Final thought:
It might be argued that, taken as a whole, the Trendy French Philosophers have created a poetic and hyperbolic—if convoluted— rejection of late 20th Century capitalist technoculture that offers little in the way of hope for that cultures' transformation or defeat. On the other hand, they are sufficiently fascinated with that which they critique to pass long hours in coffee houses, basking in their negation. As such, they serve as a tremendous inspiration to America's slackers.

Cyberpunk Lite
Gibson & Sirius Wax Laconic
Unpublished, 1994

Flashback 1989: we must have seemed to him like a bunch of over-eager yapping pups. The ascerbic, willowy, laconic Mr. Gibson was at Berkeley's superhip SF bookstore, Dark Carnival, autographing copies of Mona Lisa Overdrive, *and here he was surrounded by not less than half-a-dozen hyper grinning maniacs from this new startup magazine called* MONDO 2000.

Back then we were working on the first special "cyberpunk" issue of what we thought of as "sort of" a cyberpunk magazine. Determined we were to have interviews with Gibson and Sterling, the Beatles and Stones of the Cpunk SF movement..

We had Sterling's number and talked to him first. "Nobody wants to talk about cyberpunk anymore. We're all tired of the hype. Gibson 'll get really pissed off at you if you even mention the word. Maybe Shirley will talk to you." Eventually Synergy and St. Jude inveigled Sterling to give it up. "We've taken down the neon sign," he said, in the interview (MONDO 2000 #1), recorded by telephone from Berkeley, California to Austin, Texas. He hadn't a clue as to the sticking power of the cpunk meme.

Gibson was a harder nut. We called his book company... again and again and again. Gibson was scheduled out for his Bay Area stay, giving interviews to the established press; Chronicle, Examiner, Bay Guardian *they told us... "No! You don't get it!" we argued. "This isn't gonna be just any old 'zine. We're gonna put cyberpunk on the cover of* Time *magazine someday." (Cue the Zarathustra horns)*

The day before Gibson finally hit town, Doc Leary came through with a trump card. "You can transcribe the conversation I had with Gibson about the Neuromancer *project." (Back then Leary was involved in an association with the planned* Neuromancer *film, for whom he was to help design an interactive computer game spin-off). So when Mu bared her shiny whites in that infamous Cheshire cat grin and informed Bill that we had the goods from Leary, he seemed to become even more perplexed. He looked sorta dizzy, in fact, gripping the table in front of him and blinking his eyes. "THAT WAS NO INTERVIEW! THAT WAS A DRUNKEN BUSINESS CONVERSATION!" And so, the drunken business conversation went to press.*

Well, the years have flown by. I've only had the pleasure of hanging with Mr. G. once, for a brief time, at a VR conference. There, I turned him on to a quasi-legal smart drug which he enjoyed immensely. However, after years of mixing in similar circles, appearing in the same magazines and TV shows, and people asking me for his phone number and him for mine, it sort of felt like checking in with an old friend, when the gaunt writer strolled up to the French Hotel in Berkeley and met Bart Nagel and myself for this official book company approved MONDO 2000 *interview.*

GIBSON POPS THE WIRED QUESTION

Wiilam Gibson: What do you think about *Wired?*

R. U. SIRIUS: OK! Here we go. William Gibson interviews R. U. Sirius for *MONDO 2000* (mutual laughter). It's getting a little bit better but it's a little bit soulless.

WG: Yeah. That's what I think.

RUS: In fact, it's entirely soulless. I mean, the weird secret about *MONDO 2000* is that we're not really techno-fetishists. We're basically a bunch of freaks using the technology as a context for subversion.

WG: I know where that's at! I have alot of empathy with your position.

RUS: Us generalists take alot of shit.

WG: 'Tis true.

FATHER IS THE CHILD TO THE CYBERPUNK

RUS: What was the absolute first time you heard the word cyberpunk, as something describing someone that really existed in the culture? And what was your immediate, instantaneous response?

WG: It was in print. And I would have read it about the same time my younger colleagues, like Sterling and Shiner, would have read it. As I recall, they were rather taken with it. And I was saying, "Don't let them slap it on you! Run! Head for the hills! Don't let them put this bumper sticker on your T-shirt. It's all over now." I was quite negative about it. And I've sort of continued to be, although the bumper sticker stuck to my T-shirt. It isn't likely to go away. I just thought we were having fun, and as soon as some critic was able to apply a label it really did seem to indicate that the best part of it was over.

RUS: Do you think the label and the association with a movement resulted in your selling a lot more books? Would you have the same career if people hadn't started jumping up and down saying "Cyberpunk."

WG: I don't know. Maybe not. Cyberpunk seems to have been such a commodifiable buzz word. God knows how many pages of Sunday Supplement print has been lavished upon the word. I kind of feel like it's had its career and I've had mine and then there's some overlap. The time that I heard the name and it really made an impression was when the *Wall Street Journal* used it on the front page as a name for outlaw hackers. I thought that was really interesting. And I also thought, "Hmmm, maybe I'm free of it now." It was like "Cyberpunks Crack Computer Bank." They were obviously not talking about radical SF writers.

RUS: That's sort of what I was asking about... its escape into the real world. For awhile, you were attending lots of the Virtual Reality conferences. I saw you at Cyberthon. And then you were over in Spain with Gullichsen and Leary and...

WG: Yeah, we all had the year of living virtually. It was fun. We got to do some traveling, man. I got a free week in Venice! It seems that every country in Europe had some weird little boffin in a back room saying, (assumes German accent) "It is time to have a Virtual Reality conference now. Let's lavish thousands of dollars on having these weirdos over here." And it was interesting meeting all those VR people...

pretty odd bunch. More entertaining than meeting a bunch of Science Fiction fans. I mean, these are actual mad scientists.

DOIN' THE POMO SUBLIME

RUS: The most popular interpretation of your work is that it's dystopian. Do you agree with that interpretation?... I think it's kind of ambiguous, myself.

WG: I think my worlds look real dystopian if you're a middle class white guy doing reasonably well in 1993. But if you're crouching in a basement in Sarejevo being shelled by ethnic separatists you can read *Neuromancer* as a real escape. There are so many places in the world today that are so much crappier than anything I'm writing about. I think my work is hardly dystopian. I could imagine much worse scenarios. I don't really worry about that dystopian label too much because I think that the world we now live in is already sufficiently dire and chaotic that really straight people can't even enjoy themselves anymore. The world scares them too badly. It's pretty dystopian already.

RUS: You once said your work was about "the sense of vertigo" that you get just coping with current reality. Do you still feel that way?

WG: Oh, yeah. I get the post-modern sublime in the worst possible way... mingled ecstasy and dread.

VIRTUAL LITE

RUS: I liked *Virtual Light*, but I didn't like it as much as the Sprawl trilogy.

WG: Well, it's a different cup of tea. It's got a lot of cool stuff in it, though.

RUS: Were you, in a sense, playing to expectations with *Virtual Light*? Were you influenced by the fact that you're associated with Virtual Reality and, of course, cyberpunk...

WG: Well, yeah, to a certain extent. I was making fun of it. Other than being what it is on the surface—a kind of near-future Elmore Leonard novel, it's got a couple of other agendas. And one of them is to go back and poke fun at the more humorless elements of my technophile audience. Also, to kind of deconstruct the trilogy.

RUS: But actually this book conveys more sympathy. There's a really strong feeling of sympathy for the "bridge people."

WG: Oh yeah. I dig that kind of environment. I have a fondness for autonomous zones.

RUS: I like the fact that the guy who starts it is agendaless. You could have easily put alot of ideology into it. Bruce would've put more ideology into it.

WG: Bruce would've put more chaos theory in it. I put a little bit in. The Bay Bridge becomes the strange attractor for these folks and one night it just goes over the top and a new sort of order is established.

RUS: The description of the drug, Dancer, was a little bit unsatisfying. I wanted to know more about the experience. I noticed you put "thio" into the chemical name.

WG: Yeah, it's not very accurate. I just picked that for the ring of it. I should have come up with something really horrific. The implication is that it's more in the amine range but singularly relentless. Fast acting...

RUS: You imply a tremendous effect on the nervous system... like tarantula venom.

WG: (Laughs)... yeah, tarantula venom... something that would induce clinical psychosis really quickly by the second time you did it.

What is this? A Poem?

RUS: So what's the deal with Agrippa? Should that be viewed as a media prank?

WG: errrr.... it was an exploratory process. We made it up as we went along and we were just kind of curious to see what the outcome would be. And the outcome was that somebody cracked it and put it up on the Internet. Today, anybody can get a free copy off the internet.

RUS: I figured that it was thrown out there as a challenge and you knew it would be cracked eventually.

WG: The guys who wrote the encryption program viewed it as a challenge. So we put these two forces up against each other. We found these guys who said, "Yeah, we can encrypt this thing and nobody'll get it." But the guys who cracked it were your kind of people. They were young and crazy and into this stuff. Apparently they did quite a good job. As soon as it was out, it took them only three days to crack it open and pop it out onto the net.

RUS: This was like an attempt to reverse that whole postmodern idea that everything is trivially copied and that the value of the original artifact is obsolete. And here's this thing where you're saying that you have to buy the artifact. And just to rub our noses in it, you make it a computer-based artifact, where these postmodern rules are really supposed to hold sway.

WG: Well, that was definitely an aspect of it. Another thing that I thought was an even more playful and sadistic prank or joke is related to the serious art market and collectors. So here's this artifact and because it's going to fuck itself up the first time you read it, if you're a collector, you can't read it. If you read it, you've ruined your copy. But if you got it for speculative purposes and you go to sell it to somebody else, how can you prove to the buyer that it hasn't been used? The only way you can prove it is by running it and destroying it. I have to say, I thought that was a really nice twist, because the sort of people who were up for buying this $1500 version were speculators. They wanted to buy a couple of them, put them away, and sell them later for more. But I was quite ready to surface a couple of years later and say, "But how can you tell it hasn't been used?" (laughs)

RUS: So it sounds like you never wound up selling copies of it.

WG: Well, the publisher got into some kinds of trouble with it. There are a few. There's a couple of them in museums. A couple of people own them.

RUS: Was it originally your idea, or was it a mutual invention of several people?

WG: Dennis (Ashfather?), this painter friend of mine, sort of originated it. He did the DNA etchings. It's a shame that you never got to see the actual finished thing because it was a very cool artifact. It's extremely peculiar. In the finished form, the etchings have been xeroxed over on a big format xerox machine in a process that prevented the stuff from adhering. So when you open the box, there are these images there. But as soon as you even tilt it upright, they start sliding down and it destroys that intricate level of work, it destroys the permanence. So it's this really expensive work of fine art that's like in disappearing ink.

RUS: So where does this exist?

WG: I think the National Museum in Washington has one. And some other museum in New York. I haven't really kept track of them. I know that I don't have one myself. That's how screwed up it got.

I have a really fond memory of the night I was sitting working at my computer when the text came out of the fax machine, accompanied by a little header that some guy had downloaded on this bulletin board in New York which was his brief exchange with the anonymous guy who cracked it. It was quite charming. It said, "EUREKA! I'VE GOT IT!" (mutual laughter) And then somebody says, "What's it look like." And he says something like, "Jesus, it's weird. What is this? A poem?" .

The whole thing was a weird abstract exercise in PR. I learned alot about how strange people can get if you tell them that you're doing something but you don't want to talk about it.

Enquiring Minds want to Know

RUS: So you wrote a song for Deborah (Harry). Chris (Stein) called up all excited about it.

WG: Chris is an interesting guy. I get the feeling that he leads the kind of life that I wanted to lead when I was like fourteen. He's got all the monsters and model kits and nazi daggers a boy could want. Anyway, I wrote a bunch of lyrics and they took a bit from it and used it. It's OK. It's sort of a blues poem actually. I've heard alot of the stuff Debbie and Chris do just to get themselves off and it's astonishingly weird and wonderful stuff. She's under alot of pressure to turn in a bunch of "Blondie" music, but she doesn't really want to. They have some wild ideas for things they'd like to do. They sent me a tape once of Deborah Harry singing an invocation to Legba for an anthropological recording of a voudou ceremony. It's totally cool too because it's totally electronic. It's called "Invocation to Papa Legba" and it's got this drum chorus that sounds like six million electronic drums. It's really a great great thing! And Deborah is singing this incredibly weird and difficult traditional track. I think that sort of thing is more where her heart's at these days.

BART NAGEL: Has Billy Idol contacted you?

WG: OH NO NO NO NO NO NO NO.... (laughter). I was able to say, up until a couple of days ago, "Well, I haven't heard the album *(Cyberpunk* by Billy Idol), but I met the guy and he's OK." But now that I've heard it I just (starts laughing) don't know what he's thinking of.

RUS: You want to be nice because he's a likable guy...

WG: Yeah, ya try to be nice... (laughter). I had lunch with him once at (Faxmeals?) on Sunset Boulevard, which is an open air restaurant and I was really impressed with his patience with autograph hunters. I said to him, "Man, you have a really strange job. Writers don't have to put up with this kind of stuff." And he said, "Well, Hollywood is Disneyland and I'm one of the Mickey Mouse figures and they pay me a good wage." That made me like him very much. He has a nice sense of humor. People ask me what do I think of the record. I think from now on I'm going to say, "I think

150

it's much more interesting than Pat Benetar's record Gravity's Rainbow." (mutual laughter)

I have a stack of tapes and CD's at home that are all from people trying to do "Neuromancer, the record..." I get lots of soundtracks for *Neuromancer*. I have to say that many of them are much closer to the mark than Billy Idol's *Cyberpunk*. Much closer.

RUS: Whatever happened to the movie of *Neuromancer*? I've talked to at least like four different people in Hollywood who claim they have the rights or are about to get the rights to it...

WG: I have the rights to *Neuromancer*. I have my own plans for it, sort of. I think I'll just let it sit there while the technology matures a bit and gets a bit less expensive. I mean, you could make it now but it would cost $150 million. Maybe you could really do it up right in a few years for a lot less money.

RUS: I heard that there was this lady who bought it and was trying to turn it into a 1930's detective story...

WG: Huh?

RUS: I heard that from Tim (mutual laughter)...

WG: Oh... well I understand what he was talking about, though that's a Learyesque way of putting it. I mean, it wasn't like there were a bunch of really horrible people trying to ruin it or anything. But I got tired—in the five years it was out there—of seeing it sort of traipsing all over the world basically producing nothing but a bunch of funny stories. What I'm more into at the moment is the version of *Johnny Mnemonic* that I'm trying to do with Robert Longo, the painter and sculpture.

RUS: Robert Longo as director?

WG: Yeah...

RUS: WHOA!!!!

WG: We've been talking about it for like four or five years and it's very close.... well, you know Hollywood... it's actually pretty close. If it works, it'll be like a $40 million dollar film. With Longo, you know it's at least gonna look amazing. We get along really well that way. We have this sort of ongoing dialogue about the art direction. Really what I need to get my rocks off in film—I don't really care that much about the screenplay, I'm satisfied with the one I've written—but I really want is to be involved in the art direction. But the stuff that Longo and his production guys have come up with is so great. Like the low techs are tattooed with circuitry, they have these full-body suits that are like these circuit board diagrams. It's very nice even though it doesn't have too much to do with the original fiction.

RUS: It would be great to see this done artfully 'cause there's so much grade B cyberpunk now, like *Demolition Man* and that one with Jagger...

WG: Originally, the idea we had was for a $4 million art movie. But somehow it just grew and grew. And as more money gets into it, it gets dodgier whether or not you're able to hang on to the part of it that you like, because you have to provide something so that the viewers in like Taiwan won't feel ripped off... you have to have a certain amount of buttkicking. Although it's already violent to a fault. It's quite a violent movie. It's only got one gun, but the substitutes are quite horrific. I worked in every non-explosive projectile weapon that I've ever heard of. Everywhere you go there's this big sign, a revolver in a circle with a slash through it. So this is a world where guns are absolutely *verboten* and the only one who has one is the head of the Newark, New Jersey branch of the Yakuza. (mutual laughter) He has it in this elaborate ivory coffin locked in the back vault.

RUS: People are getting creative with homemade projectile-firing guns lately. Mark Pauline has...

WG: Yeah!!! What about potato guns? Did Mark Pauline invent the potato gun? I had a weird flash...

RUS: He talks about using soda cans though... full.

WG: He had one at SIGGRAPH in Las Vegas a couple of years ago. The thing that delighted him about it was that he'd been allowed to carry it on the plane. Anyway, somebody downloaded the plan for the potato gun on the Internet for me. I thought about building one but decided not to 'cause I have a 15 year old son. Longo said the same thing. You know that if you do it, the kid will get ahold of it.

RUS: That would make a good *Beavis and Butthead* episode. (mutual laughter)

WG: I faxed it all over the world. I figured everybody needs to know how to build a potato gun. I mean a really powerful projectile weapon that can be powered by spray mist! Talk about the street finding its own use for things, man.

Speaking of guns, I came through an airport in Frankfurt, Germany during the Gulf War and it was really interesting. We got to see the Germans laying on the kind of security they can do when they want to. I just remembered thinking, "Boy, I'm glad we're not fighting these guys." They were tooled up. They had some fancy personal hardware. These Austrian machine guns, these unbelievable kinda Star Wars guns that look like khaki plastic water pistols, and the magazine is sticking out of the front of the rifle and looks like some sort of cyborg arm... the trigger is right up by the muzzle and it has a very tiny muzzle diameter. Of course, I didn't want to go right up and look at it but I wondered what it shot. Weapons now, if they show any metal, are old-fashioned. The modern ones look like expensive tennis rackets. I looked at alot of prototypes for 21st century assault rifles while working up the armaments for *Virtual Light* and the scariest one did look like one of those Katmaster water pistols, totally plastic looking. Available in colors too. You can get yellow ones, pink ones...

The Tyranny of Hip

21•C Winter 1995–1996

not that i wasn't happy to get bailed, oh yes, but Connie is very strange. when i bolted out the cop doors to get to the open sky she was still trying to tell me about kangaroo penes. (yes, she used the real plural— penis, penes) but i already KNOW about kangaroo penes — they're double headed and furry. well!

in fact, some avant-guys are talking about getting their penes split now — split along the midline, with the heads splayed out to either side, i guess to imitate native australians, who do it to imitate the roos. if you do it, and let it heal up, and you still want to have sex, it's a terrible hassle inserting the result, but it's spozed to be worth it to both inserter and insertee.... plus it's so Hip... i guess.

NEVAH underestimate the tyranny of Hip.

sitting here in the Big City i can hear the voice of the Zeitgeist plainly, and it's a querulous male voice, and it's whining.... okay, i got it tattooed with indigo stripes and i got the ampallang shoved through, and the prince albert threaded in the top, and i got the row of ittybitty rings stapled all along the bottom... And now i've gotta take it back and have them do WHAT?????

from How to Mutate & Take Over the World *by R. U. Sirius & St. Jude*

I'm in Rapid City, South Dakota to speak to a convocation of newsweeklies. I'm staring idly out of my hotel window, thinking vaguely that the football player-type room service dude who just brought up the bottle of wine had given me one of those "Hey weirdo faggot I'd like to stomp your ass" looks that small-town rednecks do so well. When suddenly, many many feet below me, a group of goths skate by. Two boys and two girls, black clothes, multicolored hair, bleached white faces, black death lipstick... the works. I have this eerie feeling that I'm back in San Francisco, but no. This is South Dakota. This is the middle of nowhere. And I'll bet you that if I went down and talked to them, they would evince the same level of sophistication, the same passive nihilism, the same artistic pretensions, and maybe even be able to score the same quality heroin, as a S.F. goth. Or a goth from anywhere. But I take no solace in the presence of hipster tribes in Bumfuck USA.

THE CIRCLE JERKS

A subculture or counterculture enters pop culture as an idea, a meme, a set of values and—hopefully—a challenge to all that is. Punk, in 1977, was delivering an electrical shock to the laidback sleeping hippies. The industrial music subculture took punk and married it with the noise of machines and the aesthetics of computers, carrying with it a seemingly sophisticated ideology involving the use of shock, horror, Lautreamont-type visions, and Artaud-style theatrics. But let's examine this a moment.

A reading of *The Industrial Culture Handbook,* published by Re/Search in 1984, reveals an extraordinary similarity between all of the non-conforming artists interviewed. They all want to shock their audience out of complacency. They all quote from Lautreamont, Aleister Crowley, De Sade and Manson. They are all anarchists who are fascinated by fascism and serial murder. They all wear black. They all love to hate and hate to love. And, not surprisingly, they've attracted around them a subculture of people who feel exactly as they do. So the artists involved in the industrial culture, far from shocking their audience out of their complacency, now have an utterly complacent audience that gets exactly what it expects. They know that an industrial band is going to involve a particular loud drum machine rhythm and distorted vocals about angst and violence. They know that an industrial art performance might involve semi-dangerous mechanical eruptions and explosions. If you want to shock an industrial culture audience out of its complacency, show up dressed in a pink clown suit and sing Donovan songs. They will *hate* you for it.

This Subversive Moment
Arthur Kroker has aptly labeled this (post)historical moment as "the recline of Western Civilization." One aspect of that recline is the impossibility of evoking the will necessary for movements for social change. In its place, we have trends and subcultures, mini-revolts into style. Some of these trends project images of revolt that are far more extreme than those imagined by the most radical anarchists of earlier times. And, indeed, some of these subcultures may eventually turn towards actual ACTS of murderous nihilism. But even these acts will be essentially passive, not directed towards provoking radical change but directed towards amplifying the mediated pose of real cool extremism with real cold blood.

Still, there is a value in subcultures or identity tribes. In the early 1970's, for instance, we had the bisexual transgressive notion— the understanding that there was something beautifully queer about rock culture. The notion was carried forward by the New York Dolls, Lou Reed, David Bowie. It became the first post-hippie subculture, called glam or glitter. It lasted just long enough to normalize the formerly transgressive. From that moment on, lipstick boys could find a place in pop culture. But glam as a subculture disappeared.

In other words, a meme—a small philosophical virus—needs to be able to attach itself to an identity in order to spread. The identity democratizes participation. Those infected can buy the clothes and the CD's and hang out in the right clubs. People have been authentically changed, challenged, liberated into new thoughts, new behaviors, and new aesthetics by hippies, punks, ravers, queers, and even   headbangers...

Only to get imprisoned by a whole new set of expectations. If you want to transcend subculture tribalism and open yourself to constant evolution and novelty, remember these words, first uttered by Morgan Russell back in 1989: Question Authority Sez Who?

A Guy with a Backache

A guy with a backache seems like an appropriate ending to this examination of "The Life and Work of R.U. Sirius." I am indeed a guy with a backache, and I would probably do twice as much written work if I didn't have such a damned hard time getting anywhere near comfortable sitting in front of the computer.

R.U. Sirius Interview 01   Winter, 1995

Q: How do you envisage the future?
A: I take a deep whiff of ketamine and netsurf while watching cable TV. The near future of America is like a Charles Dickens novel with really cool technology. It's like *Neuromancer,* but with a shitty government AS WELL AS scary corporations and a mercenary entertainment subculture. Deeper into the 21st century, we'll be mutating, changing form, ramping up our nervous systems, growing transgendered intelligent third arms, making copies of ourselves, all that... if we make it alive.

Q: How much strong and secure would you feel inside it?
A: I'm already in it. I feel like an exile in the future that I predicted. I feel like a dispensable lowlife piece of lumpenproletariat shit...

Q: Are there any fears in confronting new forms of pain and pleasure?
A: I'm pretty straight forward on this. I fear the pain. I don't fear the pleasure.

Q: What do you miss mostly in today's world (concept, value, state, machine, anything) ?
A: I miss the belief in a politics based on desire and sexual liberation. I miss the middle period of media technology, before attention was so completely decentralized. I miss sharing the zeitgeist with millions of youths. I miss the possibility of having the kind of importance that a Lennon or a Dylan was able to have in another time. I miss hip elegance. (I think you still have this in Europe). But I only miss these things a little bit. Mostly, I'm a full-steam-ahead kind of guy.

Q: Can you describe the visions *MONDO 2000* reflects? Are they connected to present or future environments? Do they concern us or the future readers?
A: *Mondo 2000* is about the present culture. The confusion comes in NOT because *Mondo* is futurist, but because it's SURREALIST, and doesn't always conform to notions of journalism.

Q: Where is technology headed today, (if it's certain that it's headed somewhere)?
Technology is headed in all sorts of directions but the two most important ones

a) the wiring together of the human species by information and communications technology, leading ultimately to metamedia communication replacing our mouths and tongues. Virtual Reality will be how we "speak" to each other.
b) Self replicating technologies. First, information economics as the metaphor. Biotechnology as the first manifestation. Nanotechnology makes the revolution. Is being able to make infinite copies of anything you want inflationary?

Q: What is the most promising form of science according to your opinion?
I said it already. Nanotechnology or death. It's more than just a good idea, it's the law.... sloganeering is a science now too...

Q: Can anyone define eternity through technology (without losing it)?
"Define" and "eternity" might be contradictions in terms. You can EXPERIENCE eternity through certain psychedelic drugs, on a good night. You can then try to hang onto it through life-extension technology or by trying to find a hole in time or something.

Q: What do you consider your biggest success?
Launching the notion of a cyberculture, the idea that computers are creating a culture and that culture is "hip" is pretty major league I guess, although I figure it's being coopted by the suits and the reactionaries. I hope that my next book, *How to Mutate & Take Over the World,* will disturb everybody in the culture. That would be a great accomplishment.

Q: Which fictional characters would you picture yourself to be?
Combine Marcello Mastriani's role in Fellini's *8 1/2* with Jagger's role in Nicholas Roeg's *Performance.* Toss in elements of Groucho Marx AND Harpo... Notice, it's all films rather than books...

Q: Describe yourself in a few words.
A: A guy with a backache. Uh... clown prince of the 90's zeitgeist? Writer and conceptual artist? Fake media cyberpunk? A guy with a backache.

Q: What do you think about politics? Do you think that those who control the new multimedia industries will be tomorrow's leaders?
A: I find politics endlessly fascinating, and observing the political trends fills me with unmitigated anger, disgust and bile. I'm AFRAID that the new multimedia industries will in fact be the leaders. Welcome to the United Gates of Amerika. These sorts of people are little dictators. They have no notion of freedom or human rights whatsoever if it impacts negatively on their desire to build empires. The sort of people that *Wired* puts on their cover, the heavies of the new corporate media, like Redstone from VIACOM and Paul Allen of Microsoft... these people should be EXECUTED not glorified!

I'm a LEFT libertarian. I hate the arrogant kill-the-poor right libertarianism being pushed by the "A" list of the cyberculture.

Q: How do you see the situation in Europe? Does "European" in that great European Economic Corporation sanctify the victims (romanticism, idealism, children in Yugoslavia...) of present day wars?
A: You could probably tell ME more about that. Neither devolution of the state (Balkanization) nor world unity works in the current context. I've always had the weird delusion that any hope in this world was actually up to us here in the United Gates of Amerika. We'll make the cornucopia, maybe with the Japanese...

Q: Do you like TV? Do you think that VR will be the TV of 2000? What do you prefer?
I like to watch TV. I like NOT having to be interactive sometimes. And, sure, immersion will replace television eventually.

Q: What do you think about the cyberpunk culture? Is it still alive?

A: I don't know that it ever WAS alive. It was always more like a metaphor for a general trend linking Do It Yourself anarchic hipness to technology. THAT is still alive. Cyberpunk, the word, is something I can take or leave.

Q: Do you think that the hacker/cracker ethics still live inside the Internet chaos?

A: It doesn't in any sense dominate the medium anymore. My god, the whole world culture, dominated by market interests, is moving in. Hacker ethics exist in those with hacker ethics. The net, in fact, will be legislated and censored very soon, with arrogance for all from the USA, which is very far from hacker ethics...

Q: Is Internet a fashion?

A: A trend. Were telephones and automobiles once a trend? Eventually it becomes ubiquitous and the novelty and romance dissipates.

Q: How do you explain its success?

A: Beats the postal service AND the neighborhood bar.

Q: What do you think about the indie music scene? About pop cultures like grunge and techno?

A: It's all part of a tendency throughout the twentieth century for more and more people to become active communicators. Eventually, every garage will be a multi-media "corporation," each with its own spin on post-modernity. Or maybe not. A good percentage of people will probably head for post-tech zones.

As far as genres like grunge or techno or industrial or whatever, I HATE conformity, including subculture conformity. I'm a genre bender.

Q: Which movie would you have liked to direct or compose its soundtrack?

I'd like to have directed Andy Warhol's *Chelsea Girls*. I'd like to do a soundtrack for Fellini's *8 1/2*.

Q: Favorite current movie?

A: *Pulp Fiction*.

Q: *MONDO 2000* is one of the most popular new magazines in Greece, together with *WIRED*, although both written in English. How do you explain its world-wide success?

A: *Mondo* anticipated the trajectory of worldwide culture, it's beautifully designed, and it has an irreverent and paranoid wit. Who could resist?

Q: Do you mind about these new magazines copying *MONDO's* layout?

A: No. I wish that *Time* magazine would thank us regularly though.

Q: What do you often dream about?

A: Sex with teenage girls. Floating around. I seem to wind up hanging out alot with Sylvestor Stallone in my dreams, and he's always alot more fun than you'd think.

Q: How is an ordinary day of your life in S.F.?

I wake up around 9:30 am. I drink three strong cups of coffee and read the *San Francisco Chronicle*. I go on-line and pick up my email and post on whatever topics I'm active in. I make a billion phone calls, write, give interviews... whatever. I eat dinner around 8 pm. I think about going out, or seeing a girlfriend. I decide I'm too tired. I watch cable TV until 1 am and go to sleep.

Q: How do you imagine absolute happiness?
A: A harem. World revolution. Unimaginable novelties occurring with great frequency. A year off. Reversing my age back to about 20.

Q: What makes you sad? What makes you cry?
A: Women on the verge of a nervous breakdown. They make me laugh also.

Q: Do you believe in God?
A: I don't believe in believing.

Q: What is the message you like to spread through your magazine?
A: Question authority. Question people who go around saying question authority. Always cede to the humorous deflation. Fuck Newt Gingrich. Be fast. The rules don't apply to Mondoids.

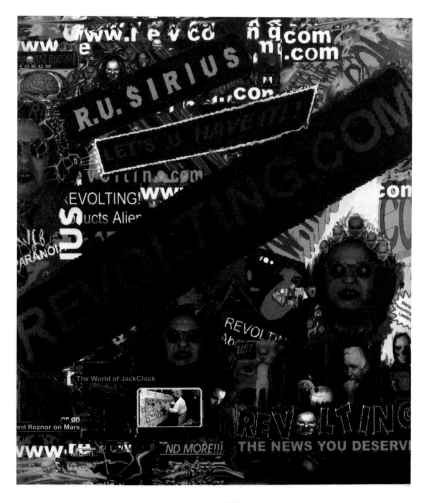

R.U. Sirius is available for public appearances, freelance writing and editorial gigs.

R.U. Sirius
P.O. Box 196
Mill Valley, CA. 94942
rusirius@well.com
~~www.the-revolution.org~~

Eve Berni
can be found at:
www.videobrain.com